W9-AGZ-798

## MODERN NATIONS
## OF THE
## WORLD

# JAPAN

DISCARDED
HEGGAN PUBLIC LIBRARY

## TITLES IN THE MODERN NATIONS OF THE WORLD SERIES INCLUDE:

Brazil
Canada
China
Cuba
England
Germany
Greece
India
Italy
Japan
Kenya
Mexico
Russia
Somalia
South Africa
South Korea
Sweden
United States

MODERN
NATIONS
—OF THE—
WORLD

# JAPAN

BY PATRICIA D. NETZLEY

Margaret E. Heggan Free Public Library
208 East Holly Avenue
Hurffville, New Jersey 08080

LUCENT BOOKS
P.O. BOX 289011
SAN DIEGO, CA 92198-9011

*With thanks to George Faber, whose
research material proved invaluable.*

Library of Congress Cataloging-in-Publication Data

Netzley, Patricia D. 1943–
    Japan / by Patricia D. Netzley
        p.   cm. — (Modern nations of the world)
    Includes bibliographical references and index.
    Summary: Examines the land, people, history, politics, and culture of
Japan and discusses its state of affairs, and place in the world today.

    ISBN 1-56006-599-0  (lib.bdg. : alk. paper)

    1. Japan—Juvenile literature.  [1. Japan.]  I. Title.   II. Series.
    DS806.N418  2000
    952—dc21                                                   99-37253
                                                                  CIP

No part of this book may be reproduced or used in any form or by any
means, electrical, mechanical, or otherwise, including, but not limited to,
photocopy, recording, or any information storage and retrieval system,
without prior written permission from the publisher.

Copyright © 2000 by Lucent Books, Inc.
P.O. Box 289011, San Diego, CA 92198-9011
Printed in the U.S.A.

# CONTENTS

# Introduction

## A Unified People

The island nation of Japan has maintained many of its ancient traditions while taking advantage of modern technology. For example, many of its people own televisions, stereos, and computers, yet they also might visit public bathhouses, partake in ancient tea ceremonies, and eschew electronic calculators in favor of the abacus, a counting device that uses sliding beads to add and subtract. This blending of ancient and modern ways led Japanese sociologist Kato Hidetoshi to write, "Japan is a country that permits the harmonious coexistence of old and new. Japan's very existence and functioning have been built upon this harmony."[1]

### Resistance to Change

Because the Japanese people value their traditional ways, they have a strong national identity and are resistant to outside cultural influences. In fact, at many times during the country's history, the Japanese have deliberately and aggressively shut out foreigners, and they have persecuted those who espoused Western beliefs. Even when Japan has accepted the practices of outsiders—either by choice or by force, as happened after World War II—the country has done so without altering the essential Japanese spirit.

Cultural changes come slowly in Japan, if at all, and can be superficial in nature. One example of this superficiality is the way the country abandoned feudalism. During the 1800s Japan officially ended the lord-peasant relationship. However, the feelings associated with this relationship—loyalty, respect for authority, the idea that one must take care of subordinates—were transferred to the employer-employee relationship. Consequently, vestiges of ancient feudalism can be found in modern Japanese corporations.

### High-Tech Success

Resistance to cultural change has not prevented the Japanese from developing new technologies and producing goods

*The abacus is an ancient Japanese device used for addition and subtraction.*

that other nations want. In economic matters, Japan is more than willing to study business techniques and adopt them, providing they do not compromise Japanese values. Scholar Boye Lafayette De Mente, who has lived in Japan and is an expert on its affairs, says:

Having been intimately involved with Japan since the late 1940s, I can attest to one difference [between the United States and Japan] that goes beyond any facade and is a vital factor in Japan's transformation from an isolated feudal society to a major economic power in just a few decades. Immediately after Japan's doors were opened to the West in the mid-1850s, the Japanese began to stream abroad on official government-sponsored, as well as independent, study-missions, seeking to absorb and synthesize everything the West had to offer. This activity was to continue for generations . . . [and] Japanese interest in . . . studying every attitude, every action . . . is as strong now as ever. . . . In contrast, most Westerners not only remain almost totally ignorant of Japan and things Japanese, they show little real interest in learning.[2]

## AN ANCIENT APPROACH TO MODERN PROBLEMS

The Japanese have studied American society, and when necessary they have cooperated with the United States to improve their own nation. But even while functioning as part of the international community, the Japanese have not allowed Western ideas to alter their cultural attitudes. De Mente notes that this is in keeping with an ancient Japanese philosophy called *kyosei,* which he defines as "living in cooperative harmony with the rest of the world."[3]

Harmony is highly valued in Japanese society, as is self-discipline. The ability to control one's mind and body is considered a necessary skill, and the American tendency to blurt out one's feelings is considered a weakness. Consequently, the Japanese approach to social issues is very different from that common in the Western world, using a traditional mindset to deal with modern problems. Therefore the national character has remained unchanged for thousands of years, even though many Japanese have adopted some of the trappings of American life.

# The Impact of Geography

Japan's geography has heavily influenced its national identity. The country is a chain of over three thousand islands stretching northeast to southwest and isolated from its nearest neighbors—Korea, China, Russia, and the Philippines—by the Sea of Okhotsk to the north, the Sea of Japan to the west, and the East China Sea to the south. To the east is the Pacific Ocean and across four thousand miles of water the North American continent.

This lack of shared borders has enabled the Japanese to control the influx of foreign goods, people, and ideas into their lands. As scholar Richard Tames explains:

> Above all, Japan has had the blessing of isolation and thus freedom from the constant invasions which have so dramatically shaped the history of its Asian neighbours. The adoption of foreign ways has been a formative element in the evolution of the national culture, but the process has usually been voluntary, selective and gradual. It has also been conscious. Foreign visitors and goods have never, since Japan began to achieve statehood around the fourth century A.D., silently penetrated across frontiers undetected but arrived a few at a time and visibly, by ship.[4]

## Mountainous Terrain

The Japanese people are also cut off geographically from one another. Most islands have high mountains that divide the land into many small blocks, separating east coast from west. Like the country's lack of close neighbors, this too has affected national attitudes. As Professor Sakamoto Taro, an expert on

Japan's ancient history, points out, the country's "mountainous, confined topography" is one reason why the Japanese
have a "strongly exclusivist, sectional attitude, and the tendency to give birth to small, regional governments."[5]

Over 70 percent of Japan is mountainous. The reason for such rugged terrain lies in Japan's geologic origins. Its islands are actually the tops of mountain ridges that arise from the ocean floor. These ridges continue to move because Japan remains subject to orogenic (mountain-building) forces such as earthquakes and volcanoes. In fact, the country is situated on one of the largest and most active earthquake faults in the world. Minor earthquakes are an almost daily occurrence, and major earthquakes are a constant threat.

## EARTHQUAKES AND VOLCANOES

The most recent major quake struck on January 17, 1995, and killed over 5,000 people in the city of Kobe, about three hundred  miles southwest of Tokyo. However, it was not the most severe earthquake in Japan's history. That title is claimed by the great Kanto earthquake, which took place on September 1, 1923. It killed over 140,000 people and destroyed 70 percent of the city of Tokyo, largely because it was followed by a massive fire. Other earthquakes have caused tidal waves, or tsunamis, that rise up from the sea to destroy coastal communities.

Violent volcanic eruptions also occur frequently. The country has 60 volcanoes that have been active at some

*Mount Fuji, the highest peak in Japan.*

point in history, or one-tenth of the world's active volcanoes. There are also about 150 inactive volcanoes or volcanic formations. Of Japan's 24 highest peaks, 8 are dormant volcanoes.

The highest of these, Mount Fuji (12,388 feet), was once extremely active, emitting a constant plume of smoke and spewing ash on a regular basis. After an eruption in 1701, however, it became dormant. Now it only occasionally releases steam from a small vent.

Meanwhile, several new volcanoes have formed during the twentieth century, including Showashinzan on Hokkaido and Myojin-sho off the Beyoneisu Rocks in the Pacific Ocean. Most of Japan's volcanoes—whether new or old, active or inactive—have steep slopes. The surrounding areas typically have many basin-shaped depressions called calderas, which often develop into lakes.

In fact, most of Japan's lakes are volcanic in origin. Others form in depressions left by earthquakes or are created when sandbars close off the mouths of bays. Some lakes are born when valleys flood. But regardless of how they developed, most lakes are fairly small. The largest lake in Japan is Biwa on the island of Honshu, which covers over 260 square miles. There are also many short, fast, steep rivers, which contribute to the ruggedness of the landscape by eroding mountain faces and carving small valleys and plains. Rivers originating in volcanic areas carry acidic water and cannot be used for irrigation, drinking, cooking, or bathing.

## CLIMBING MOUNT FUJI

Over two hundred thousand people try to scale Mount Fuji, the tallest mountain in Japan, each year during the official two-month summer climbing season. At one point, the climb was considered a sacred pilgrimage, and mountaineers still traditionally pray for good fortune before beginning their climb. Along the way they stop at several "stations" that dot the mountainside. Each station has several huts where climbers can buy food, drinks, and canned oxygen at high prices. Some of the huts have beds for napping. The path upward is lined with crushed lava rocks, but the terrain is difficult nonetheless, and many give up before reaching the summit 12,388 feet above sea level.

## CLIMATE

In addition to volcanic activity, Japan is threatened by typhoons, serious tropical storms that primarily occur in August and September. Typhoons often cause massive floods, landslides, and damage from heavy winds. There is also a rainy season in June and July, when it rains almost daily, as well as scattered rain throughout the rest of the year.

Most areas receive over 40 inches of rain per year, although Japan's rainfall totals vary widely depending on location, as does the amount of snowfall. For example, on the island of Honshu, one mountainous region gets over 160 inches of rain per year, while the city of Tokyo gets only 60 inches. Similarly, Tokyo gets only a few days of snow in the winter, while the island of Hokkaido gets 130 days. Snow is particularly heavy along the Sea of Japan. In fact, this region has some of the deepest winter snow in the world.

Winter temperatures also vary dramatically, from daytime highs of fifteen degrees Fahrenheit in the north to forty-five degrees in the south. Summer temperatures range from seventy degrees in the north to eighty degrees in the south. The reason for such temperature variance lies in Japan's length. Over thirteen hundred miles from north to south, its island chain stretches from the subarctic zone to the subtropic zone.

East-west differences in climate exist as well, but for a different reason. Japan is only about two hundred miles wide at its broadest point, so longitudinal variations are small. However, because of the country's mountainous interior, each coastline is subject to different winds. In addition, Japan lies in a region where air masses coming from Asia mix in the upper atmosphere with those coming from the Pacific Ocean. This can cause sudden changes in climate, particularly during spring and fall.

## VEGETATION AND WILDLIFE

With its abundant rainfall, Japan has lush vegetation. Nearly two-thirds of Japan is covered with forests, and these regions offer a wide variety of birds and game animals. The northern islands are primarily known for their foxes and brown bears. The middle islands have wild boars, deer, antelope, bears, weasels, pheasants, mandarin ducks, and wild monkeys

Margaret E. Heggan Free Publ
208 East Holly Avenue
Hurffville, New Jersey 08

## AVERAGE MONTHLY WEATHER

| | Tokyo Temperatures | | | | | | | Sapporo Temperatures | | | | | |
|---|---|---|---|---|---|---|---|---|---|---|---|---|---|
| | F° | | C° | | Days of rain or Snow | | | F° | | C° | | Days of rain or Snow |
| | High | Low | High | Low | | | | High | Low | High | Low | |
| Jan. | 46 | 30 | 8 | −1 | 8 | | Jan. | 28 | 12 | −2 | −11 | 26 |
| Feb. | 48 | 30 | 9 | −1 | 8 | | Feb. | 30 | 12 | −1 | −11 | 23 |
| Mar. | 54 | 36 | 12 | 2 | 13 | | Mar. | 36 | 19 | 2 | −7 | 23 |
| Apr. | 63 | 46 | 17 | 8 | 14 | | Apr. | 52 | 32 | 11 | 0 | 13 |
| May | 70 | 54 | 21 | 12 | 14 | | May | 61 | 41 | 16 | 5 | 14 |
| June | 75 | 63 | 24 | 17 | 16 | | June | 68 | 50 | 29 | 10 | 13 |
| July | 82 | 70 | 28 | 21 | 14 | | July | 75 | 59 | 24 | 15 | 13 |
| Aug. | 86 | 72 | 30 | 22 | 13 | | Aug. | 79 | 61 | 26 | 16 | 13 |
| Sept. | 79 | 66 | 26 | 19 | 17 | | Sept. | 72 | 52 | 22 | 11 | 17 |
| Oct. | 68 | 54 | 20 | 12 | 14 | | Oct. | 61 | 39 | 16 | 4 | 17 |
| Nov. | 61 | 43 | 16 | 6 | 10 | | Nov. | 46 | 28 | 8 | −2 | 19 |
| Dec. | 52 | 34 | 11 | 1 | 7 | | Dec. | 34 | 18 | 1 | −8 | 25 |

called the Japanese macaque. The southern islands have many snakes and hares.

The waters around Japan were once similarly rich in wildlife, including sea turtles, whales, dolphins, and many types of fish and crustaceans. However, overfishing and pollution have depleted the ocean's bounty in modern times. Consequently, whereas the Japanese once fished only in coastal waters, during the 1960s they began to venture further into the Pacific Ocean and as far away as the Atlantic Ocean. When other nations objected to the Japanese coming close to their shores, Japan negotiated fishing agreements that allowed them to continue the practice.

At the same time, the country developed aquaculture, which is the farming of seafood such as shrimp, scallops, and oysters. Although this brings much additional food, it is still not enough to meet Japan's needs. The country is now one of the world's largest importers of marine products, receiving seafood primarily from the United States, China, Taiwan, and Korea.

## A SELF-SUFFICIENT PEOPLE

During its early history, Japan refused to trade with foreigners to obtain food. Therefore, although flat land was scarce and soil generally poor, the Japanese people developed farming techniques that made their acreage highly productive, and they learned not to waste food. Their housing construction techniques also took full advantage of limited space. Moreover, a room used for sleeping at night was always used for other purposes during the day. In this and other ways, Japan's geography forced its people to be efficient and frugal.

Japan's resistance to foreign interference was made easier because of the country's natural barriers, which include not only mountains and seas but also some extremely rugged coastlines. No trader could enter the country without alerting the populace, and Japan could defend its shores with little difficulty. In contrast, countries on the Asian continent, such as China, had to deal with encroachment along many miles of shared borders.

Therefore the Japanese people developed a different mindset than the Chinese. As early as the third century A.D.,

## THE WHALING INDUSTRY

Japan objects to current bans on international whaling because the activity has long been important to the Japanese people. Whaling was a major coastal industry in Kyushu beginning in the mid–sixteenth century, supplying jobs and food to many people. At first whalers used harpoons, but in the late seventeenth century they devised special nets to make their catch. During the next 130 years, they killed over 21,700 whales. The carcasses were processed on land, and no part of them was wasted. Bones were used as fertilizer, baleens and teeth as hairpins and combs. Whale hair was employed to make rope, whale hide to make glue, and whale fat to make whale oil. Tendons became bow strings or other weapons, and ambergris was processed into perfume. In contrast, Western whalers used only the baleen, ambergris, and the parts of the whale necessary to make whale oil; even the meat was often wasted. Meanwhile the Japanese relied heavily on whale meat as a source of protein. From 1930 to 1940, it accounted for 15 percent of all the meat eaten in Japan, and during the post–World War II food shortages this figure rose to 30 percent. School lunches also featured whale meat until the late 1960s, when the global community began to restrict Japanese whaling.

Chinese visitors to Japan were commenting on these differences, describing the Japanese avoidance of foreigners and their reluctance to leave home. A few centuries later, Japan's government decided to close off its country completely to outsiders, officially forbidding foreigners from visiting its islands and citizens from leaving.

## A RISING POPULATION

Because so few people left Japan and the country was relatively peaceful, its population grew rapidly. According to some scholars, by the seventh century it had already reached 5 million people and by the fourteenth century it was 10 million. There are currently about 125 million people in Japan, which makes it the seventh most populous country in the world.

It is also one of the most densely populated countries. Approximately 98 percent of Japan's 145,882 square miles of land is on four main islands—Honshu, Hokkaido, Kyushu, and Shikoku—but because of the country's mountainous terrain, the Japanese live on less than 10 percent of this amount. Four-fifths of the population, or approximately 100 million, inhabit the island of Honshu, which is also the largest island geographically. Hokkaido has only 5 percent of Japan's population, while the island of Kyushu has about 12 percent and Shikoku has less than 4 percent.

Because of its large size and population, the island of Honshu is divided into five socioeconomic districts: Kanto, Kinki, Chubu, Chugoku, and Tohoku. Of these, the most heavily populated is Kanto, with 30 percent of Japan's people. It is also the district where the capital city of Tokyo is located. The Kinki region, where the major cities of Osaka, Kobe, and Kyoto are situated, has 18 percent of the people, while the Chubu region has 17 percent. Chugoku and Tohoku are far less populated, with only 6 and 8 percent of the population, respectively.

Tohoku was also once the home of the Ainu. These people were the earliest inhabitants of Japan, but during ancient times they were attacked by the ancestors of modern Japanese, who had invaded the islands from Asia. By the Middle Ages, most Ainu had been killed, assimilated, or driven north to the island of Hokkaido. Today 99.4 percent of Japan's people are ethnically Japanese. Most of the remainder are Korean, numbering about 700,000 people; there are only about twenty-five thousand pure Ainu left in Japan. The majority of Ainu live on the island of Hokkaido, where there are approximately one hundred small Ainu villages.

*Japan is the seventh most populated country with 125 million people.*

### SMALL ENTERPRISES

Hokkaido is also known for its agricultural concerns. All of Japan's main islands have some form of farming. On Honshu, for example, the region of Tohoku supplies the country with 70 percent of its apples and 25 percent of its rice, which is the country's principle crop. However, Hokkaido has the largest agricultural establishments, with twenty-five- to fifty-acre farms a common sight.

*Tokyo, the capital city of Japan.*

On other islands, most farms are extremely small, and farmers receive a substantial portion of their income from second jobs. This is also true for the fishing industry. Most fishing businesses are run by families or individuals, despite government efforts to encourage large organizations, and fishing income is often supplemented with other work.

Similarly, the mining industry is composed of many small, scattered mines rather than large concerns. In part, this is due to the uneven distribution of mineral deposits as well as Japan's difficult terrain. Coal, for example, is primarily accessible only on Hokkaido and Kyushu. Moreover, Japan's mineral resources are generally not plentiful enough to meet its people's needs, which means that as the country became industrialized it had to engage in trade.

Today the country imports approximately 70 percent of its raw materials, including fossil fuels, textiles, timber, lumber, chemicals, food, and metallic materials. Its exports are primarily manufactured goods such as automobiles, machinery, and electronics. Japan is responsible for 10 percent of the world's exports, and its main customer is the United States. There is a serious trade imbalance in this regard; the U.S. trade deficit with Japan reached $64 billion in late 1998, and in early 1999 the United States warned Japan to stop flooding the U.S. market with steel.

## FEUDAL BEGINNINGS

Industrialism turned Japan into a major economic power. It has also been responsible for the creation of several important cities. For example, Nobeoka and Minamata on the island of Kyushu grew up in response to the region's raw materials and fast-moving rivers, which provide hydroelectric power and create a perfect location for manufacturing.

However, most Japanese cities originated in response to the feudal system that existed in early Japan. Under feudalism, the lord of a powerful family would build a castle, and his supporters would live in the surrounding area, called a fiefdom. The stronghold would then attract merchants and craftsmen, and eventually a city would emerge. This pattern of development is the reason that only the United States has more cities than Japan, even though the latter is geographically smaller. Records indicate that as early as the first century A.D. there were over a hundred fiefdoms in Japan, and for

## YAMATO TAKERU

The son of an emperor, Japanese folk hero Yamato Takeru might have lived in the second century A.D., when he supposedly expanded the territory of the ruling Yamato clan. His exploits during this period are told in two chronicles, *Kojiki* (A.D. 712) and *Nihon Shoki* (A.D. 720). In one story, Takeru disguises himself as a woman in order to kill two warriors at a banquet in his honor. In another he uses a sword to cut his way through a grassfire. Takeru is said to have died from an illness, whereupon he turned into a white bird and flew away.

several centuries this number continued to grow.

Prior to the fourth century A.D., each feudal lord functioned independently. Then one of the larger fiefdoms, held by the Yamato clan, began absorbing the rest. By the end of the fourth century the Yamato had unified the country, establishing an empire and setting itself up as the imperial family that still holds the Japanese throne today. Japanese legend reports that emperors existed as early as 660 B.C., but it was the Yamato who created a true dynasty with a hereditary ruler and a centralized government.

### POLITICAL INFLUENCES ON LAND MANAGEMENT

The Yamato court was comprised of members of two factions within the country, the *Muraji* and the *Omi*. The former was a group of clan families that had always supported the new emperor. The latter was a group of equally powerful families that had sworn allegiance to the new emperor after his throne was established. All heads of state came from these groups.

Until the sixth century, the Yamato court was unstable, with struggles from both within and without over who would succeed the throne. This changed when Prince Shotoku took over the throne as regent for his aunt, Empress Suiko, after her husband was murdered. Shotoku was a popular leader who had many new ideas and was not hesitant to implement them. For example, he opened relations with China and sent Japanese students there to study. He also encouraged the spread of Buddhism, the prevalent religion of mainland Asia, and strengthened ties with the Korean state of Paekche, which first introduced Buddhism to Japan. In addition, Shotoku established a more orderly government, creating specific court ranks and outlining government duties, responsibilities, and rights in a constitution.

Shotoku brought stability, but after his death in 622 the country was thrown into turmoil. Shotoku's son, Yamashiro Oe, succeeded him, but the powerful family of Empress Suiko, the Soga clan, murdered Yamashiro Oe in 643 and took over the throne. Two years later the imperial family killed the Soga and their supporters and regained control of the country.

In 646 the court sought to strengthen its position by abolishing private land ownership. All farms immediately became the property of the government, which redistributed it to every male over the age of six. Each land allotment was roughly the same size, but the most productive plots were typically given to high-ranking officials and other important people. All tenants had to pay taxes on the land, regardless of their status in society, in exchange for the right to cultivate it.

*Prince Shotoku established relations with China and sent Japanese students there to study.*

At first, goods were accepted as payment; later the government began minting coins so that its people did not have to rely entirely on the barter system.

The imperial court instituted many other changes as well, which collectively became known as the *Taika* (Great Change) reforms. The most significant was the establishment of a new political system based on geographical units. It identified over sixty provinces called *kuni* or *koku,* which contained a balance of mountains, coastal plains, and interior valleys. Each *kuni* was divided into districts called *gun,* each encompassing several villages or *ri.* Administrators called *richo* governed the *ri,* overseen by the *gunji* who governed the *gun* and the *kokushi* who governed the *koku.* The *richo* and *gunji* were selected from important local families, but the *kokushi*

## FORMS OF ADDRESS

The Japanese use language to honor an individual's social standing. There are three levels of politeness used in addressing someone: the colloquial, the neutral, and the honorific, or *keigo*. Japanese speak in *keigo* to those of higher social status, such as teachers, elders, customers, employers, and, of course, the emperor. Verb forms are different for each level of speech, as are many vocabulary words expressing the same ideas. In addition, some words are only used by women, others by men. In addition, when writing names, the Japanese typically put family names first and personal names last. However, modern Japanese increasingly write their names in the Western style, with the family name last. In writing about historical figures, they usually honor the tradition of putting the family name first, but not always. Moreover, prior to the 19th century, only noblemen and samuri had family names; everyone else had only personal names. This makes the issue of Japanese name order very confusing.

were government officials who had to meet strict educational requirements and were reevaluated yearly.

The *kokushi* also supervised public works projects. Labor for such projects was provided by slaves, who at the time made up one-tenth of Japan's population, and by farmers, who were required to serve the government for a maximum of sixty days per year. This service could include military duty.

### DEFENDING THE LAND

The imperial court did not develop a permanent army because it lacked foreign enemies. However, in A.D. 660 Japan became involved in a military action when it sent troops to aid Paekche, the Korean state that had brought Buddhism to Japan years earlier. Paekche was being threatened by China and neighboring Korean states. These combined forces eventually proved too powerful for the Japanese, who retreated and then fortified their lands closest to Korea, fearing retaliation.

Meanwhile more reforms were being implemented. The government built a road system, carried out a census, and drew up new laws. In 710 it also established Japan's first permanent capital city. Prior to this time, the imperial family had designated a new capital each time a new emperor took the throne, believing that a ruler's palace had to be abandoned upon his death to avoid bad luck. Now the court designated the city of Heijo (later called Nara) as Japan's capital, intending it to remain so forever. However, in 794 the court moved the capital to Kyoto, and in 1868 it moved it to Tokyo.

In building its first permanent palace, the imperial family was heavily influenced by Chinese architecture. Many aspects of Chinese culture were being adopted in Japan during this time, including etiquette, arts and crafts, and the Chinese system of writing, although eventually all of these would become uniquely Japanese. Meanwhile, Buddhism continued to spread. Supported by a succession of emperors, at first it was embraced only by the upper classes. The lower classes remained loyal to Japan's native religion, Shinto, which worshipped gods representing various aspects of nature. Gradually, however, the practice of Buddhism became more common, although it did not entirely replace Shinto.

During the same period, the population of Japan grew rapidly, and as each male reached the age of six he expected to receive his portion of land to farm. This meant that the government had to identify and distribute new farmland at a rapid rate. In 743, the court decided to reduce its burden by decreeing that anyone who found and cultivated his own plot could have permanent private ownership of it. This new policy was immediately abused by the leading clan families, who worked several plots of land at once in order to amass large private holdings. This brought them additional wealth and power, and they started maintaining their own armies to protect their land and control the peasants who farmed it for them.

Soon a few large clans once again began to rival the strength of the imperial family. At this point, just as when Japan had hundreds of fiefdoms instead of one empire, the country decided to isolate itself entirely from foreign influences. In 884 the imperial court officially cut all ties with China. Japan was once again an island both geographically and psychologically.

# 2

# FOREIGNERS AS ENEMIES AND REFORMERS

In the ninth century, Japan entered a period of isolationism that would last approximately two hundred years. The government successfully eliminated all foreign influences, believing them detrimental to society. Nonetheless, it remained threatened by enemies within the country.

## THE SAMURAI

The primary threat was from regional clans with large land holdings. Wealthy and powerful, their lords kept large armies of professional warriors who were first known as bushi and later as samurai. These warriors eventually comprised a separate social class, passing their status down from father to son, or if the son was deemed unworthy, to sons-in-law or nephews.

Over time, the warriors' families became clans more powerful than those they served. Nonetheless, the samurai remained loyal to their lords, because it was part of the samurai code, or Bushido, to do so. This code dictated the behavior of every member of a samurai's family, both male and female. In addition to feudal loyalty, it demanded that its adherents obey certain customs, train in martial arts, and commit suicide when captured by an enemy or dishonored.

A samurai's duties varied according to the needs of his lord. Many enforced tax collection and maintained public order. Some also engaged in warfare against other samurai, either on behalf of their lords or for their own warrior clans. The system of mandatory military service for Japanese farmers had been abandoned in 792, so the samurai were needed to keep the peace. In addition, all official redistributions of land ended in 844, which meant that a lord or samurai who wanted additional land often had to fight for it.

*A samurai warrior collected taxes and maintained public order as well as engaged in warfare.*

## THE TAIRA AND THE MINAMOTO

In 935, one warrior clan, led by Taira no Masakado, conquered almost all of the Kanto provinces, and by the last part of the twelfth century it had seized control of Kyoto from another powerful clan, the Fujiwara. For centuries the Fujiwara had enjoyed enormous influence in the imperial court, advising a succession of emperors and encouraging them to marry Fujiwara women. Once the Taira clan had usurped the Fujiwara, the Taira also married into the imperial family and awarded themselves large estates.

In addition, the Taira killed dozens of their rivals. One of the people they executed was the head of another warrior clan, the Minamoto. Like the Taira, the Minamoto clan had gained power throughout the tenth and eleventh centuries,

## THE BELIEFS OF THE SAMURAI

The code of the samurai, or Bushido, can be understood through quotations from great warriors:

"The man whose profession is arms should calm his mind and look into the depths of others. Doing so is likely the best of the martial arts."—Shiba Yoshimasa (1350–1410)

"Without knowledge of Learning, one will ultimately have no military victories."—Imigawa Sadayo (1325–1420)

"No matter whether a person belongs to the upper or lower ranks, if he has not put his life on the line at least once he has cause for shame."—Nabeshima Naoshige (1538–1618)

"A man who has been born into the house of a warrior and yet places no loyalty in his heart and thinks only of the fortune of his position will be flattering on the surface and construct schemes in his heart, will forsake righteousness and not reflect on his shame, and will stain the warrior's name of his household to later generations. This is truly regrettable."—Torii Mototada (1539–1600)

"In strategy your spiritual bearing must not be any different from normal. Both in fighting and in everyday life you should be determined though calm. Meet the situation without tenseness yet not recklessly, your spirit settled yet unbiased."—Miyamoto Musashi (1584–1645)

and during this time it allied itself with the Fujiwara clan. When the Taira executed its leader, the Minamoto clan supported the efforts of that man's son, Yoritomo, to exact revenge. Led by Yoritomo's cousin, Yoshinaka, and half-brother, Yoshitsune, the clan successfully drove the Taira from the capital and later destroyed them in a dramatic sea battle.

In 1185, Yoritomo established a military government in the town of Kamakura, appointing military governors called *shugo* to oversee activities in all of Japan's provinces. He also appointed military stewards, or *jito*, to collect taxes, supervise public and private estates, and maintain public order. In 1192 the emperor officially awarded Yoritomo the title of shogun, or general-in-chief, of the entire country. This marked the beginning of a military dictatorship that would last for almost seven hundred years. Called a shogunate, it gradually took over all functions of the government, leaving the emperor a power in name only.

Yoritomo died in 1199, but the Kamakura shogunate continued under the leadership of the Hojo family, to which Yoritomo had been related through marriage. Their position was weakened, however, by Mongol military invasions during the late 1200s. Although these invading forces were defeated—largely because of destructive typhoons rather than warfare—the expense of the military actions drained Japan's coffers. At the same time, the typhoons were seen as divine winds, or kamikaze, and united the people in the belief that they were special to the gods.

With depleted fortunes, the Kamakura shogunate was taken over by the Ashikaga family in 1333. Five years later, an Ashikaga was named shogun and moved the headquarters of his new shogunate to the city of Kyoto. The Ashikaga shogunate remained in power there until the 1500s, but only with much difficulty. Threats on the government were common, as

*In 1192, Yoritomo was awarded the title of Shogun, or general-in-chief, of the entire country.*

was warfare between large clans throughout the country, and for a period of sixty years, a second court with a rival emperor challenged the shogunate.

Although the unification of these two courts was negotiated in 1392, disputes over successions to the throne continued. The country's economic troubles continued as well. Consequently in 1467 a civil war broke out. It lasted ten years and further weakened the Ashikaga shogunate, which collapsed in 1573. Thirty tumultuous years later, the Tokugawa clan established a new shogunate to replace it.

## THE TOKUGAWA SHOGUNATE

The Tokugawa shogunate lasted 264 years, from 1603 to 1867. During this time the government again promoted strict isolationist policies. In 1635 it forbade its citizens to travel to other countries, expelled most Europeans from Japan, and sought to stamp out foreign influences on its culture. In the mid-1500s, traders from Portugal and Jesuit missionaries from Spain had begun visiting Japan. These visitors were welcome at first, but soon the Japanese became mistrustful of them, believing that the foreigners planned to take their land and might send armies to conquer them.

The Japanese government also objected to the spread of Christianity, fearing that this new religion would obliterate their traditional way of life. Consequently in the late 1500s Japan ordered all missionaries to leave the country. Those who refused were executed, along with Japanese Christians who refused to renounce their new faith.

Religious persecution continued into the 1600s, when entire villages of people were forced to step on pictures of Jesus or on other religious icons in order to prove they were not Christians. Often, those who would not do this fled to avoid execution. In 1637, a group of about forty thousand Christians barricaded themselves in a fort in Kyushu, where they held off government attackers until the following year. When at last their fort was overrun, all of them were killed.

## A UNIQUE CULTURE

For the next two hundred years, Japan let no foreigners into the country, with the exception of a few Dutch and Chinese traders who were restricted to one port on a small island near Nagasaki. This period was relatively peaceful but also restrictive. The Japanese adhered to a rigid social structure, and family members were expected to display absolute obedience to the head of the household, just as warriors showed obedience to their lords. Loyalty was emphasized, in part so that people would believe it immoral to undermine a superior. Distinctions between social classes were also strictly enforced.

During the Tokugawa shogunate, approximately 80 percent of the people were farmers, 7 percent warriors, and the remainder merchants and artisans. Though their numbers were relatively small, these merchants and artisans became increasingly influential in Japanese society. The merchants in some industries, such as sake brewing and money lending, formed themselves into large business concerns to which the warriors often became indebted. In addition, urban merchants heavily supported the arts.

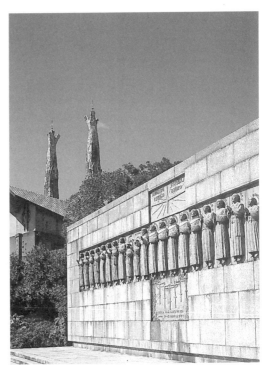

*A monument dedicated to the Japanese Christians who refused to renounce their faith.*

Puppet theater was particularly popular, as was a type of live acting called Kabuki drama. Paintings depicting city scenes, actors, and courtesans were also in demand. Dyeing and weaving were improved, as were decorative painting and pottery techniques, and flower arranging and the tea ceremony became a more important part of Japanese life. In fact, schools devoted to the latter two activities were established throughout Japan during the Tokugawa shogunate.

## FLOWERS AND TEA

Flower arranging, or ikebana, in Japan has always been very different from flower arranging in Western countries. The Japanese believe that a person engages in ikebana not only with the intent of creating a beautiful display but also to attain a connection with heaven and earth and to develop internal strength and discipline. When the arrangement is finished, each flower should appear to be alive and in perfect harmony with its surroundings. During the Tokugawa shogunate, ikebana was practiced by both men and women,

## THE CATHOLIC MISSIONARY

A Roman Catholic missionary from Spain, Saint Francis Xavier (1506–1552), is credited with bringing Christianity to Japan. He was the third son of a nobleman who ordered him to pursue a career in the ministry. Consequently he was sent to Paris to study theology in 1525. However, he did not become passionate about his faith until 1534, when a roommate, Ignatius Loyola, convinced him and others to take a solemn vow of poverty and pledge to devote their lives to saving souls. Xavier pursued the priesthood and in 1537 he was ordained. Shortly thereafter he went to Rome to serve the pope, who eventually assigned him to convert the Asian subjects of King John III of Portugal to Christianity. Xavier spent from 1542 to 1545 in India, then went to the Malay Archipelago and the Spice Islands. During his travels he met and converted a Japanese man who convinced him to go to Japan. He traveled there on a Portuguese ship in 1549 and converted thousands of Japanese before returning to India in 1551. Xavier intended to go back to Japan after visiting China, but while awaiting approval for his journey from the Chinese government he took ill and died. He was considered a saint even before his death, but was recognized as such by the church in 1622. He was named patron saint of missions in 1927.

but today it is primarily a female pursuit. There are over twenty major ikebana schools still in existence.

Like ikebana, the tea ceremony was a part of Japanese culture prior to the Tokugawa shogunate but became more intricate and widespread during this period. There are several tea ceremony styles, but as with ikebana, all forms of the ceremony are intended to promote internal harmony and discipline as well as to express beauty and perfection. An attendant at many tea ceremonies, Boye Lafayette De Mente describes the basic procedure as follows:

> Any conversation before the ceremony begins should be light and calm and designed to enhance a contemplative, serene mood. Once the guests have all arrived, and the time is right, the host ladles powdered green tea into each guest's cup in turn, pours hot water over it, and then uses a whisk to stir it to a foam.

The taste of the tea is astringent. It is meant to stimulate the taste buds and help the person feel alive and at one with nature and the universe.

Once the tea is drunk, the guests take turns commenting on the beauty of the tea cups and expressing their appreciation to the host for the hospitality.

An essential part of the tea ceremony is scrutinizing and appreciating the utensils used. . . . The various items are passed one at a time to each guest, who is expected to demonstrate both taste and refinement in commenting on and appreciating the beauty and artistry of the implements.[6]

However, some people believe that modern expressions of the tea ceremony have lost the intent of the ceremony that originated during the Tokugawa shogunate. For example, Peter Popham and Bradley Winterton, two British authors who have written extensively about Japanese culture, acknowledge that the earliest forms of the ceremony had numerous rules, but argue that these rules did not inhibit the communal spirit of the event. They say:

*Japanese women preparing tea.*

The tea ceremony was not really a ceremony at all—it was just a tea party. A small group of friends gathered in surroundings they considered congenial, brewed and drank tea and talked. Great care and discernment went into the choice of everything used at the party: the tea-making utensils and bowls, the tea itself, . . . the accompanying cakes. . . . The conversation, too, was well-considered and tasteful and revolved around the objects used or the beauties of the season. Silence was also permitted.

The object was to enjoy, in a brief space of time and in simple surroundings, a fragment of eternity; to allow one's true nature, usually buried under noise, activity and desire, to come out and bask in tranquility. . . . The naturalness and friendliness which must have played a part [in ancient times] have been exorcized, and the ceremony, now truly ceremonious, is performed on stage and presented as if on a velvet cushion for the edification of visiting celebrities.[7]

### AN INTEREST IN LITERATURE

The Tokugawa shogunate promoted an appreciation for nature and beauty. It also furthered the spread of knowledge. Commercial publication began in 1609, and shortly thereafter, public demand for literature dramatically increased. At the same time, woodblock printing in colors developed, so books began to have lavish illustrations.

The first Japanese history book was the *Kojiki,* which appeared around 712. The first novel was printed in the tenth century. Written by noblewoman Murasaki Shikibu, it was entitled *Genji monogatari (The Tale of Genji)* and deals with a prince who romances a variety of women. Other novels with romantic, courtly heroes soon followed, relying on a format similar to *Genji monogatari.* However, during the Tokugawa shogunate many new novel genres developed, such as the *otogi-zoshi,* or fairy-tale book, and the *ukiyo-zoshi,* or "floating world" novels. The latter presented stories about people whose main pursuit in life was pleasure. Novels also increasingly concerned the lower classes rather than concentrating on life at court.

This change in focus was due in part to the fact that more people in the lower classes were learning to read. Along with an increase in literature came an increase in literacy. As Ed-

 **THE PILLOW BOOK**

One of the earliest Japanese books is *The Pillow Book* by Sei Shonagon, a lady-in-waiting to a tenth century empress. The title refers to the fact that Sei hid a diary in her pillow, which was actually a wooden neckrest, in which she wrote comments about life at court, sayings, thoughts about nature, lists of likes and dislikes, and other musings. Sei's work began a literary genre called *zuihitsu,* or "running brush," in which authors shared random notes about life. Some of the advice in *The Pillow Book* includes: "Oxen should have very small foreheads," and "A priest ought to be good-looking."

win O. Reischauer explains in his book *The Japanese,* during the Tokugawa period the samurai became "men of the writing brush rather than the sword."[8] By the end of the period, most of the warrior class were literate, as were all but the poorest of peasants.

## COLLAPSE OF THE SHOGUNATE

An increasing number of people from all classes devoted themselves to scholarly study, particularly of Chinese Confucian doctrines. These doctrines had been introduced into Japan in the twelfth century but were largely ignored by the populace. In the Tokugawa period they received a great deal of attention, not just in major cities but throughout the countryside as well.

During the Tokugawa shogunate, government leaders, intellectuals, and students often traveled between cities and rural villages. Therefore new ideas spread easily from one place to another. As a result, according to Reischauer, the Japanese "became culturally more homogeneous and developed an extremely strong sense of national identity."[9]

Nonetheless, as Confucianism became prevalent, the Japanese people became interested in the Chinese way of life and began to question their own. In particular, they wondered whether having a shogun as a leader was good for their country. China was ruled not by a military dictator who controlled a shadow emperor but by a strong emperor making decisions alone. Consequently criticisms of the shogunate increased, and Japanese literature began to extol the virtues of divine rule.

But despite such criticisms, the Tokugawa shogunate remained relatively strong until the United States established contact with Japan. In 1853, an American fleet of warships went to Edo Bay (now Tokyo Bay) to force the Japanese to open their borders to trade. This resulted in a limited treaty, and five years later a more extensive agreement was struck with the help of Great Britain, which also threatened Japan. Treaties with other foreign traders soon followed.

Each alliance with an outsider resulted in a new round of criticism of the shogunate by the Japanese people, who believed that their military government should have done more to protect the country from foreign interference. Passions ran high, shogunate officials were assassinated, and the people clamored for the full power of the emperor to be restored. In 1866, the Emperor Mitsuhito ascended the throne at the age of fourteen. When the shogunate collapsed in early 1868, Mitsuhito reestablished absolute imperial rule and at his coronation took the name Meiji, which means "enlightened government." He ruled until his death in 1912, and this period became known as the Meiji Restoration.

## MODERNIZING THE COUNTRY

The Meiji emperor made many changes in Japan. For example, he established a modern banking system and the yen-based monetary system that is still used today. He built lighthouses, ports, railroads, a telegraphic network, and mining operations. He instituted a new, mandatory school system. He formed a strong centralized government, with ministries, a cabinet, a constitution, a parliament called the Diet, and a modern legal system. He also reestablished the emperor's control of all lands, making the lords into regional

*American warships in Edo Bay force Japan to open its borders to trade.*

## THE MURDERED HEIR

In 1592, the warrior Toyotomi Hideyoshi adopted his nephew, Toyotomi Hidetsugu, and made him his heir. At the time, Hideyoshi controlled the government through a position as the emperor's *kampaku,* or chancellor. The young Hidetsugu took over this position, and at first he did a good job. Then he grew arrogant and corrupt, and after a while Hideyoshi became disgusted with him. Still, Hidetsugu might have remained in his position of power had it not been for the fact that Hideyoshi finally had a natural son in 1593. After the baby was born, Hideyoshi forced his nephew from the capital in disgrace and eventually encouraged him to commit suicide. Then he had Hidetsugu's three young children killed, along with thirty women in the Hidetsugu household. Hideyoshi died in 1595, leaving a two-year-old boy as his heir.

governors and abolishing class distinctions. In particular, he ended the samurai class, which had enjoyed many special privileges, and replaced it with a conscript army.

Some of these changes were not fully accepted by the Japanese people. For example, there were several samurai uprisings during the Meiji Restoration, the largest and last in 1877, as well as many political upheavals while the new Diet, cabinet, and military struggled to determine their roles in governing the country. Nonetheless, Japan prospered. During the late 1800s and early 1900s, the country experienced industrial growth and gained new territories through wars with China (1894–1895) and Russia (1904–1905). By the end of World War I, Japan had taken over significant parts of the Asian mainland and controlled Taiwan, Korea, and several other islands.

The Meiji emperor died on July 30, 1912, and was succeeded by a mentally ill son, who was soon replaced by his own son, Crown Prince Hirohito. Hirohito was named emperor on December 25, 1926. His reign experienced perhaps the most difficult challenges of Japan's history.

Just three years after Hirohito became emperor, an economic depression struck the Western nations, which in turn decreased Japan's profits from trade. The country's silk industry was hit particularly hard, but other businesses suffered as

*Yen, Japanese currency.*

well. Foreign goods became scarce and costly. In an attempt to change their country's fortunes, the Japanese decided to increase their territories to acquire new natural resources. In 1931 they took over Manchuria and subsequently ignored Western demands that they return it to the Chinese.

## THE RISE OF THE MILITARY

This show of strength boosted public support in Japan for the military. As a result, the army was gradually able to take over Japan's government, and a general was appointed Prime Minister. At the same time, Japanese forces continued to take over parts of China, and in 1940 Japanese troops occupied French IndoChina, now known as Vietnam. By this time, World War II was raging in Europe, and Japan had signed pacts with the aggressors in that conflict, Germany and Italy. The United States therefore began to perceive Japan as a threat and blockaded oil shipments to its ports. Japan countered by bombing Pearl Harbor, the Hawaiian stronghold of the American navy in the Pacific, on December 7, 1941.

The United States then declared war on Japan, but with much of its Pacific fleet destroyed, it could not prevent the Japanese from quickly taking over the rest of Southeast Asia and much of the surrounding region. By the middle of 1942, Japan controlled the Philippines, the Dutch East Indies, Malaya, Burma, almost all of the islands in the central Pacific, and part of Alaska's Aleutian Islands.

However, Japan's victory was short-lived. The attack on Pearl Harbor had not destroyed any of America's aircraft carriers, only battleships, and U.S. forces were able to use these carriers to launch several successful attacks on Japanese forces. In May and June of 1942, Japan lost decisive naval battles in the Coral Sea and off Midway Island, and shortly thereafter the Japanese government fell. America then launched a series of bombing raids on Japanese cities and industries, and on August 6, 1945, the United States dropped an atomic bomb on the city of Hiroshima. Three days later another bomb was dropped on Nagasaki.

*The USS Arizona as it sinks during the bombing of Pearl Harbor.*

Japan is the only country ever to have been bombed by an atomic weapon, and the result was devastating. Both cities were almost totally destroyed, leaving over two hundred

*The aftermath of the atomic bomb that was dropped on Nagasaki.*

thousand people dead, several hundred thousand injured, and untold more suffering from radiation-related illnesses that would not show up until years later. Even before the bombings, Japan had essentially lost the war, but afterward the amount of destruction forced the country to accept its defeat and surrender.

## RECOVERING FROM DEFEAT

From the Depression through World War II, the Japanese had experienced widespread poverty and food shortages. In fact, daily life was so difficult that today the Japanese call this period *kuraitani,* or "valley of darkness." But at the end of the war the future looked no better. Throughout the country, over 1,855,000 Japanese were dead, and approximately 678,000 were wounded or missing. Roughly one-third of the country's industrial equipment had been destroyed, along with one-quarter of its buildings and most of its ships. Moreover, under the terms of its surrender, Japan had to dismantle its military and agree to be occupied by its former enemies.

The Japanese people feared that these occupying forces, which were largely American, would treat them badly. Instead the United States helped Japan rebuild its country and instituted a number of political, educational, and social reforms designed to establish a democracy and prevent Japan from resuming its militaristic ways. For example, the United States ended Japan's feudal system by enacting land reforms that broke up large agricultural concerns into many small, individually owned farms. The United States initiated the same type of breakup of Japanese business conglomerates, or *zaibatsu,* but suspended its efforts in the early 1950s because they were threatening the economic strength of Japan.

The American occupation of Japan officially lasted until 1952. During the seven years of U.S. intervention, Japan's infrastructure was rebuilt and modernized. As scholar Richard Tames points out:

> If the war had destroyed much, it also had its positive side. Army service had introduced millions of peasants to the mysteries of the [automobile], radio, and telephone. Cameras and motorcycles made for the military could be redesigned for the civilian market. Where factories and transport systems had been demolished by

enemy action they could be replaced with new technology. Throughout history the Japanese had shown a remarkable tenacity in the face of disaster, whether it be fire, earthquake or typhoon. Now, instead of rebuilding a village, they needed to rebuild a nation.[10]

## A STRONG ECONOMY

This flurry of construction stimulated the economy. Demand for building supplies increased, and those who manufactured them profited. Other social changes, such as the reapportionment of land that created new landowners, also encouraged spending and increased wealth, which in turn enabled more Japanese to buy luxury items. During the early 1950s, so many people purchased televisions, refrigerators, and washing machines that they soon were considered a necessity rather than an extravagance. During the 1960s, sales of automobiles and air conditioners soared.

Over the ensuing years, Japanese corporations became rivals to American ones. The country had not only recovered but also prospered from its wartime destruction. Moreover, the strengths that had served the Japanese well in their early history continued to benefit their now business-oriented society. Employees were as loyal to their employers as they once were to their feudal lords, and they worked tirelessly without complaint.

From the 1970s through the 1990s, business remained the main focus of Japanese society, and crises related to the economy received far more attention than other types of problems. For example, in the 1970s, Japan's main supplier of oil, the Middle East, placed an embargo on oil shipments. Japan acted immediately to solve this problem, enacting oil-saving measures and looking for new sources of energy.

In contrast, during the early 1950s, doctors began to encounter people with strange neurological disorders. They eventually determined that the people had eaten fish from a particular bay that had become contaminated with mercury. The Chisson Chemical Company, which had dumped the mercury, disputed this fact, and the Japanese government sided with the corporation for over a decade, wanting to protect the economic interests of the country. Meanwhile, hundreds of people, especially unborn children, became crippled or died from mercury poisoning. Similarly, air pollution in Japan became extremely severe before the country began to pass and enforce laws curtailing pollution from industrial sources.

Because the economy is so important to the Japanese, business leaders often escape criticism. This sometimes leads corporate executives, many of whom have political connections, to believe they are beyond the law. As a result, during the 1990s, there were several serious scandals involving the use of bribery to influence stock prices and other business transactions. There were also many cases of political corruption. In addition, for the last few decades Japan has been accused of engaging in unfair trading practices. Meanwhile the country's economy has been growing increasingly unstable, and financial experts believe that major changes in Japanese society will be necessary if Japan is to prosper in years to come.

# 3

# A PEOPLE OF INDUSTRY

Japan is a leading industrial power, with the second largest economy in the world and roughly 60 million workers. Though the country rivals the United States in its business successes, its corporations function very differently from their American counterparts, and these differences in turn create different societal pressures. Japanese workers and their families face a unique set of problems because of the way their culture views work-related issues.

## THE CORPORATION AS CLAN

Japan's major businesses are grouped together into industrial enterprise groups that are much like families or clans. There are six major industrial groups: Mitsubishi, which is made up of 139 companies; Mitsui, with 110 companies; Dai-Ichi Kangyo, with 117 companies; Sumitomo, with 108 companies; Sanwa with 84 companies; and Fuyo with 64 companies. The Dai-Ichi Kangyo group has three subgroups: Furukawa, with 10 firms; Kawasaki, with 4 firms; and NKB, with 16 firms. There are ten lesser industrial groups: Nippon Steel, with 40 firms; Toyota, with 30 firms; Hitachi, with 38 firms; Nissan, with 27 firms; Tokai Bank, with 25 firms; Matsushita, with 25 firms; Industrial Bank, with 23 firms; and the companies of Toshiba-IHI, Tokyu, and Seibu. In addition, Japan has nine huge trading companies as well as dozens of small ones.

Although the companies within each group are independent entities, they coordinate their activities within the group to minimize competition. The six largest and oldest groups were derived from family-run industrial and financial conglomerates called *zaibatsu*, which developed during the

Meiji Restoration. Led by powerful men who expected total obedience from subordinates, they originally operated much like feudal kingdoms. Vestiges of this system remain part of their ideology today.

## LOYALTY AND DEDICATION

Large Japanese corporations traditionally employ people from the time they enter the workforce until mandatory retirement at age fifty-five or sixty. Even in the face of business setbacks, employees are rarely laid off. Russell Jones, a chief economist with a major Japanese corporation, reports: "The main way unemployment is rising is through bankruptcy—when [corporations] have no choice [but to let workers go]."[11]

 ## ADVOCATING WESTERNISM

During the eighteenth and nineteenth centuries, two important men advocated Westernism, the replacement of fundamental Japanese practices with Western ones. The first of these men was Toshiaki Honda (1744–1822), a respected mathematician and one of the first Japanese scholars to study Western culture. Honda studied the Dutch language in order to understand their mathematics, and this led him to study other Western subjects as well. Eventually he advocated ending Japanese isolationism and adapting the Western alphabet. The second man to suggest that Japan adopt Western ways was Fukuzawa Yukichi (1835–1904). The son of a samurai, he founded a large newspaper and a major university and wrote over a hundred books, most of which concerned Japan's relationship with the West. Fukuzawa learned English in the mid-1850s and accompanied the first official Japanese visits to the United States and Europe in the early 1860s. When he returned, he published a three-volume book of his observations entitled *Conditions in the West,* which gave the Japanese people many insights into Western culture. In subsequent books, he advocated that Japan adopt many aspects of Western civilization—an unpopular view that sometimes brought him threats of assassination. Gradually, however, Fukuzawa's opinions changed, and in his later years he argued that Westerners were racists who merely wanted to exploit the Japanese people and destroy Japanese culture.

Mark Magnier, a business reporter for the *Los Angeles Times,* says that this approach to employment is deeply rooted in Japanese culture: "It is around jobs, more than any other aspect of life, that the country's ancient protective instincts—embodied by powerful Japanese institutions defending their turf—are playing themselves out."[12] Therefore, despite a troubled economy, Japanese corporations have strenuously resisted factory closures and job layoffs, even when such actions are in their best interest.

In return for this job security, Japanese corporations expect employees to be loyal and highly committed, and employees generally comply. Leaving one corporation to take a job at another is rare. Instead a worker is hired at the entry level and promoted to higher and higher positions within the same company. These promotions are almost always based on years of experience rather than merit; workers hired at the same time advance at the same time, regardless of whether they perform well or poorly. In other words, the promise of lifetime employment is not dependent on performance.

Regardless of level, employees are expected to put in long hours. Many corporate employees work six days a week, stay at the office late on weeknights, and take few if any vacations. Commuters sacrifice even more hours to their jobs, particularly in Tokyo, where approximately 12 million people ride Japan Railways trains each day. This level of commitment to work, and the corresponding lack of leisure time, leads to great stress. In fact, death from work-related stress—whether due to consequent physical ailments or emotional pressures and suicide—is so common that the Japanese have a word for it: *karoshi.*

Despite such stresses, employees are expected to support their employers in public. Even in private, complaints are not encouraged. If an employee insists on presenting a grievance, under Japanese law a corporation is not required to discuss the situation with him. Instead the employee must use his labor union as an intermediary.

But labor unions in Japan are not like those in the United States. While American unions represent a particular craft or occupation (for example, teachers or steelworkers), Japanese unions represent an individual corporation. Therefore unions are often on the side of the corporation rather than the worker and generally avoid confronting business leaders. Unions also have no incentive to change the status quo. Kenichi Ohmae, a Japanese management consultant, reports that union leaders have historically been "treated very well [by corporations] and

*Approximately 12 million people ride the Railways trains each day in Japan.*

# THE RAILROAD SYSTEM

The idea for the first Japanese railroad system came from a gift from America. When U.S. Commodore Matthew Perry arrived in Japan in 1853, he gave the emperor a replica of an American steam locomotive as a gift. Built at one-quarter the size of the original, it moved along a circular track that Perry had laid down on the beach. This demonstration captured the imagination of the Japanese, who became determined to build their own railroad. In 1869 Great Britain helped them achieve their goal by giving them a loan as well as the expertise of British civil engineer Edmund Morell. Construction on the railroad started the following year, and two years after that, Japan had its first steam railway: eighteen miles of track linking Tokyo with the port of Yokohama. The engine that ran along that track, a nineteen-ton English steam locomotive, can be seen today in Tokyo's Transport Museum.

became nobility, elitists, where they worried about the good life rather than changing the country."[13]

The courts also make it difficult for an employee to gain satisfaction during a labor dispute. Work-related lawsuits can take as long as ten years to resolve, and typically the corporation is the victor. In recent years, some workers have tried to manipulate business leaders to settle out of court by shaming them. Japanese corporations cannot stand embarrassment because company image is as important to its executives as profits are. Therefore when an employee threatens to picket in front of an office or talk to reporters about bad business practices, employers often become cooperative.

However, few employees resort to such tactics because they too want to avoid embarrassment. It is considered dishonorable to make a public spectacle, so most workers keep their job complaints to themselves. Moreover, few employees will risk being fired, not only because a job loss is a cause for shame, but also because many corporate jobs come with benefits that employees do not want to lose. For example, the larger corporations provide housing for executives, either for free or at low cost, and dormitories for unmarried factory workers. Mid-level white-collar workers might receive low-cost housing construction loans. Companies also pay their workers seasonal bonuses that can equal several months' pay, and the largest corporations offer executives annual free vacations to resort areas.

*Competition for white-collar corporate jobs is severe, so only those who attend the best schools can acquire them.*

## RAISING GOOD WORKERS

Many companies also send employees to special training camps that teach team spirit through lectures and physical activities. Such training is a continuation of what the Japanese were taught as schoolchildren. Japan's educational system emphasizes the need for people to be compliant, loyal, and industrious, and nearly every student's goal is to work in a major corporation someday.

Just one hundred years ago, there was no Japanese word for "competition." Children worked at whatever job their fathers had held. Fishermen's sons became fishermen; warriors' sons became warriors. Today, however, that tradition is gone. Moreover, surveys indicate that approximately 80 percent of Japanese believe themselves to be middle-class, and with literacy now at over 99 percent, distinctions between job applicants are not as profound as in the United States. Therefore competition for white-collar corporate jobs is severe, and only those who attend the best schools can acquire them.

Most children begin school at age six. They attend six years of elementary school, three years of junior high school, three years of senior high school, and four years of university. While this structure is the same as in the United States, Japanese instructional methods are very different from American ones. Students typically learn through rote memorization and recitation, with little deviation from traditional lesson plans. Teachers are strict; classes are regimented. Most students wear uniforms, and expressions of individuality are not encouraged.

This system has worked well to turn out skilled and competitive workers. However, some experts believe it is becoming outdated. For example, Mark Magnier says, "The traditional emphasis on memorization, conformity and respect for authority now leaves graduates increasingly ill-suited to a global world of ideas and information-based industries."[14] Similarly, Japanese investor Chikara Kanzawa says, "In Japan, being the same as everyone else is safe. That's why it's hard to create innovative systems."[15]

In addition to stifling creativity, Japan's educational system typically puts its students under severe psychological stress. Japanese children study more subjects than Americans; for example, most learn to play a musical instrument and to speak English as well as Japanese. Even at the elementary-school level, Japanese students have far more homework than Americans—usually five to six hours a night—yet the Japanese spend just as many hours per day in the classroom as American students.

A Japanese student who does not perform well is never held back a grade to relearn the material. Entire classes graduate together, no one is flunked, and 95 percent of all students go through all four years of high school. However, throughout the educational process, all students are tested to determine whether they deserve to be in a good school or a mediocre one. Entrance exams are administered prior to each new level of schooling—elementary, junior high, high school, and university—and those who do poorly on these tests are not allowed to attend the most prestigious schools.

To improve their chances of success, millions of Japanese children between the ages of six and fifteen attend *juku,* or

*In Japan, students must wear uniforms, and expressions of individuality are not encouraged.*

"cram schools," each summer. There are currently over 180,000 cram schools in Japan for primary and junior high school students, with a yearly attendance of over 5 million, and over 200 preparatory schools, or *yobiko,* to help high school graduates study for university entrance exams. *Yobiko* often advertise the percentage of their former students who have passed the university exam. Those with the best rates are very expensive to attend, yet students compete for openings.

University test scores are important because students who do not get into a top university will not be hired by a major corporation. Consequently people who fail to score well on a university test may become distraught, even though they are allowed to retake it after further study. Some even commit suicide over a poor score. One Japanese psychologist explains that failure to succeed in school "is deeply associated with feelings of worthlessness, shamefulness, and alienation. All of it seems to be greatly influenced by the stereotyped sense of values in contemporary society in which a good school record and an academic career as well as sociability and cheerfulness are thought to be important."[16]

## LACK OF SUPPORT

People who want a white-collar job but cannot get hired by a major corporation must work for a medium-sized or small business. These places pay 30 to 40 percent less than large companies and offer far fewer benefits, yet they demand the same level of employee loyalty and diligence. However, loyalty is not necessarily rewarded with job security. Firings and

## THE HIGH COST OF LIVING

Tokyo is the most expensive city in the world for Americans living abroad. In 1999, food in Tokyo was more than double the price of food in New York, the most expensive city in the United States. A loaf of sliced white bread, for example was $6 to $8 a loaf, and butter was over $7 a pound. A quart of milk was $2 to $3. A movie ticket was $16.30 to $27.00, and a taxi ride from Tokyo's airport to its downtown area was $250.

layoffs are much more common outside of large corporations, and opportunities for advancement are few. Most small businesses remain small because it is difficult for them to compete with companies in corporate groups. Nonetheless, approximately 40 percent of Japan's labor force work in businesses with less than one hundred employees.

Some people choose to start their own businesses, but entrepreneurs have a particularly hard time succeeding in Japan. In part this is due to a longstanding stigma against being different, even if that difference is an economic one. Hiroyuki Tahara, a manager at Nikko Securities, suggests that this emphasis on uniformity is in part due to the fact that Japan's first workers were farmers in small communities, where the emphasis was on cooperation and sharing rather than on competition. He contrasts this with the attitude of early Americans, who remained isolated in family groups and competed with others for food. Tahara says, "The United States comes from a hunter-gatherer tradition. Japan grew up as a farm society where it wasn't good to make more money than everyone else."[17]

Entrepreneurs also face greater risks in Japan than in America. Mark Magnier reports:

> While the United States tends to admire the plucky fighter who fails three times before succeeding, Japan is much less forgiving. This can discourage risk-taking. Bankruptcies can take up to a decade to arbitrate. Top executives bear personal responsibility for company debts. Stumble, and financing quickly dries up, business colleagues shun you and even your kids may be bullied at school.[18]

## DRUGS AND VIOLENCE

Denied opportunity and individuality, some Japanese turn to alcohol and drugs. Alcohol is legal and easily available throughout Japan. There are over 225,000 drinking establishments, in addition to other places where alcohol is served, as well as many coin-operated vending machines that dispense alcoholic beverages. However, most alcohol is consumed by male white-collar workers between the ages of twenty-two and fifty-two. The most popular alcoholic drink is beer, followed by sake, whisky, and brandy.

*Sake, a popular alco-
holic drink made from
rice.*

Japan has strict laws against the manufacture, import,
possession, sale, and use of unprescribed drugs, and they are
diligently enforced. Nonetheless, illegal drug use has been
rising, with an increase in arrests of approximately 9 percent
a year. Drugs are often brought into the country by organized
gangs.

As with corporations, these gangs have a clan-like structure and are part of larger entities or crime syndicates called
*yakuza.* There are approximately two thousand major gangs
in Japan with a total of about seventy-five thousand members. Their primary activities involve victimless crimes such
as gambling, prostitution, gun running, and drug procure-
ment; they do not usually engage in robbery or murder.

Police know the identity of most gang members but do not
arrest them unless they witness them engaging in an illegal
activity. There are approximately 28,500 policemen in Japan,

7,000 policewomen, 1,215 police stations, and thousands of street-corner police posts. Also called police boxes or *koban,* these small posts appear in every city and town in Japan and have contributed to the country's relatively low crime rate.

Violent crime in Japan is particularly rare; according to 1995 statistics, less than 5 percent of the country's half-million criminal cases involve assault and less than 1 percent murder, armed robbery, and arson combined. Theft accounts for more than 85 percent of the remainder. However, violent crime is increasing among young offenders, although it is not as serious a problem as in the United States.

Some Japanese blame Western influences for this rise in violence. Many aspects of American culture are popular in Japan, including movies, computer games, and clothing. Traditional Japanese disapprove of these foreign influences, just as their ancestors did prior to the Meiji Restoration. And although it is no longer possible physically to isolate Japan from Westerners, some people believe that a psychological isolationism is necessary to maintain Japanese culture.

*A* koban, *or small police post, appears in every city in Japan and contributes to the country's low crime rate.*

## A WOMAN'S PLACE

Tradition remains extremely important in Japan, and change is not easily embraced. Therefore women have had a difficult time entering the workforce and gaining equal rights. Japan is a patriarchal society, in which men typically make the decisions and women are expected to obey them. A few women have challenged this system, but the majority of women still accept male dominance. Women politicians are rare, holding only about 5 percent of legislative seats, and out of Japan's more than seventeen thousand lawyers less than five hundred are women. Only 7 percent of all office managers are women.

Approximately 40 percent of women hold jobs outside the home. Most are technicians, salespeople, or menial workers. About 30 percent of Japanese women graduate from a university; of these the majority have taken a two-year clerical course. Women earn an average of 53 percent of what men make, and some companies refuse to hire women at all, despite laws mandating equal rights and pay for comparable work. Until recently, most women willingly quit working when they got married, but today 60 to 70 percent of unmarried women say they want to keep working after marriage. However, few married women will work unless their husbands have given them permission to do so.

About 30 percent of Japan's marriages are arranged by parents, and even when a woman chooses her own mate, she typically marries only with her parents' permission. Less than 50 percent of unmarried women say they would go against their parents' wishes in this regard. Once wed, a woman continues this subservient role. A wife's primary function in the marriage is to run the household and raise children. She does not attend business functions with her husband, nor does he bring clients or even friends from the office home for dinner. Men keep their business and family lives separate. Consequently most spend little time with their wives.

However, many married men have mistresses. Male infidelity has a long tradition in Japan, and being able to support a mistress was once considered a status symbol. Some of the most prestigious mistresses have traditionally been geisha. These women are professional entertainers who act as hostesses at male gatherings, which take place in buildings known as geisha houses or at inns or restaurants.

Peter Popham and Bradley Winterton report that while statistics on the number of geisha in Japan remain unconfirmed, some estimates put their number at around sixty thousand. These women, who wear white face makeup and elaborate hairstyles and garments, perform an important role in Japanese society. Popham and Winterton explain their purpose:

*Geisha entertain businessmen while they discuss negotiations.*

> They impinge very little on the life of the ordinary person. The true geisha is a hostess for the big shots. Traditionally and still today, despite the great increase in the number of love marriages, most male entertaining and carousing goes on outside the home and marriage and in the context of work. In Japan, business is pleasure—and, conversely, pleasure is very big business. . . . [Geishas] have spent many years learning the arts required to soothe the big shots' worried brows: *shamisen* [a stringed instrument] playing, singing, dancing. They are also adept at telling jokes, talking hilariously about nothing much and generally breaking the ice so that the

customers, who may be setting up a political deal or negotiating the sale of 100 industrial robots, feel both important enough and comfortable enough to get down to doing business with one another. Many accomplished geishas are more like mothers to their guests than mistresses, but as many as one-third are believed to be "sponsored" by one or more sugar-daddies. What they do offstage—beyond the tea house—may be as important economically as what they do on stage.[19]

Although geisha often become mistresses to important men, they are not prostitutes. Prostitution exists in Japan, but since 1957 it has not been legal. However, this does not keep the approximately five hundred thousand women currently employed in Japan's bars, cabarets, theaters, and massage parlors from engaging in the activity.

When a wife finds out that her husband has a mistress, she usually says nothing. Just as disgruntled employees rarely complain about their bosses, so too do wives rarely condemn their husbands' infidelities. Few women ask for a divorce, although rates have been climbing in recent years. In 1963, only 7.3 percent of marriages ended in divorce; by the late 1990s, that figure increased to 23 percent. In the 1990s the vast majority of women who divorced were in their late twenties or early thirties and in their first years of marriage. In contrast, regardless of age, most men who discover their wives are unfaithful divorce them.

Women also experience inequality in regard to their duties maintaining the household. They not only bear all responsibility for raising children, but must also care for elderly in-laws. Due to Japan's low birth rate and its aging population, a woman might have several elderly relatives to manage and no one to help her, even if she is married and works outside the home. This situation places a great deal of stress on women, and has become such an important issue in Japan that much has been written about it. One of the country's most popular modern novels, *The Twilight Years* by Sawako Ariyoshi, concerns a wife's struggles to care for her husband's parents.

## SAVING FACE

Both men and women must learn how to deal with modern problems in a culture that maintains ancient traditions. This is not easy, particularly in a country where stoicism is expected.

## Yanagita Kunio

Yanagita Kunio (1875–1962) was the founder of Japanese folklore studies. A graduate of Tokyo University, he worked as a bureaucrat, journalist, and poet before turning his attention to folklore around 1930. At that time, Yanagita realized that much could be learned about the development of Japanese traditions by studying the country's earliest stories. He related literary themes to national character, and established this approach as the standard for subsequent folklore research in Japan. In authoring several books on folklore, he also wrote extensively on the nature of the common man and the importance of family. Today he is revered for his devotion to Japanese culture and scholarship.

Image is very important in Japan, and it is necessary to keep one's problems private. An expert in Japanese business practices, Boye Lafayette De Mente, explains the concept of "face," or *kao,* which is behind this necessity:

> As a tightly knit, group-oriented society in which people are not free to move from one job to another, discard old friends and make new ones, or move away and start over when they have problems or fail, the Japanese are very much concerned about their face—their reputation. . . .
>
> In a Japanese company, every employee has a face that goes with his or her person and job. Because of the group orientation and consensus approach to management, the face of each person is inextricably linked to that of his co-workers on all levels and to the face of the company.
>
> People must know and maintain the face that is proper for their position. If they step out of bounds, they endanger their own face, as well as that of co-workers.[20]

Such attitudes reflect the struggle between the old and the new in Japan. The country's businesses make some of the most technologically advanced products in the world, yet its workers continue to think in traditional ways.

# 4

# An Ancient Culture in Modern Times

Although Japan is a modern nation, much of its culture honors ancient traditions. The Japanese people have not allowed foreign influences to change their beliefs, and their basic approach to life has remained essentially unchanged throughout history.

## Shinto Beliefs

After World War II, the United States occupation forces disestablished Shinto, a religion that originated in Japan at least as early as the first millennium B.C. Nonetheless, in the 1990s there were over one hundred thousand Shinto shrines and dozens of Shinto celebrations throughout Japan. Both honor local *kami,* or spirits, which represent various aspects of nature (for example, mountains, rivers, waterfalls, winds, and fire) and influential entities (such as diseases, military heroes, and emperors). The religion emphasizes an appreciation of nature and a respect for life, as well as a love of purity, cleanliness, and simplicity. People also worship *kami* to avoid misfortune.

The Japanese participate in Shinto because it connects them to their community and their land, and because they believe that the abandonment of Shinto rituals might cause them harm. The religion, which had no official founder or scriptures to express a particular dogma, does not require adherence to a strict moral code. Instead, according to scholar Paul Watt, Shinto began as "an amorphous mix of nature worship, fertility cults, divination techniques, hero worship, and shamanism,"[21] and it retains some of those characteristics today. For example, Popham and Winterton describe one way that Shinto beliefs manifest themselves in everyday life:

When the people next door to the Saitos decided to re-build their house, they went to stay with relatives nearby, but the grandmother of the house came to the site early each morning to pray to the *kami-sama* of the land to allow the operation to go through without harm. She put little cones of salt all round the site, with a lighted stick of incense in the center of each. When the old building had been demolished, a square of young bamboo trees in leaf was erected, connected by sacred rope, and a Shinto priest was called in to purify the ground. A similar ground-breaking ceremony took place at the site of a new TV factory nearby.[22]

According to Watt, the Shinto religion, although primitive, has retained its hold on the Japanese people largely because of their resistance to change. He says:

Remarkably, neither Shinto's relatively primitive origi-nal character nor the introduction of more sophisti-cated religions, such as Buddhism and Confucianism,

*Shinto priests enter a shrine at a festival in Tokyo.*

caused the religion to wane in importance. In part its continued existence can be explained by pointing to changes that took place within Shinto, for after the sixth century, it was gradually transformed into a religion of shrines, both grand and small, with set festivals and rituals that were overseen by a distinct priestly class. However, such developments have had little effect on basic Shinto attitudes and values. More crucial to Shinto's survival, therefore, have been its deep roots in the daily and national life of the Japanese people and a strong conservative strain in Japanese culture.[23]

## THE SPREAD OF BUDDHISM

In the 1990s approximately 98 million Japanese participated in some form of Shinto worship, and most homes had small Shinto shrines where people could express gratitude to the gods. But the practice of Shinto does not preclude a person from also following the teachings of Buddhism, a religion that originated in India approximately twenty-five hundred years ago. Koreans brought Buddhism to Japan during the sixth century A.D., and due in large part to the efforts of a seventh century regent, Prince Shotoku, it spread quickly throughout the country. In the 1990s roughly 88 million Japanese engaged in some type of Buddhist worship.

In order to facilitate the acceptance of Buddhism by the Japanese, its early practitioners tried to show a connection between their religion and ancient Shinto beliefs. They often built their temples on sacred Shinto ground and suggested that Shinto deities and Buddhist bodhisattvas were essentially the same entities. In the process of linking these two faiths, the first Buddhist monks in Japan created new forms of their religion more suited to Japanese culture, and Shinto and Buddhism came to be widely viewed as two paths to the same religious truths. Consequently most Japanese today practice both faiths.

There are currently over seventy-seven thousand Buddhist temples in Japan. They represent many different sects, each with its own writings and tenets. Buddhists disagree about how to interpret the teachings of the religion's founder, Siddhartha Gautama (also called the Buddha, or "Awakened One"). Generally, however, all Buddhists believe that an individual will continue to be reincarnated, lifetime

after lifetime, unless he or she achieves a level of enlighten-
ment known as Nirvana. Nirvana can be attained by practic-
ing eight precepts that include Right Speech, which involves
speaking clearly and kindly; Right Livelihood, which involves
choosing an occupation that promotes well-being; and Right
Mindfulness, which involves self-examination and self-
awareness.

One type of Buddhism, Zen, has had perhaps the most influence on Japanese culture. It was adopted by the samurai
warriors and shoguns who ruled Japan from the early 1200s

*One of the seventy-
seven thousand Bud-
dhist temples in Japan.*

to the mid-1800s. Zen includes a strict regime of meditation that encourages complete self-control. Zen Buddhists believe this discipline will help them achieve Nirvana.

### CONFUCIANISM

While many Japanese try to live according to Buddhist beliefs, many also follow Confucianism, a system of social ethics that is often mistakenly called a religion. Confucianism originated in China in the sixth century B.C., and like Buddhism it was introduced into Japan by Koreans during the sixth century A.D. The system emphasizes respect for authority. Under Confucianism, people are expected to acknowledge the wisdom of older generations, honor tradition, and demonstrate absolute obedience to one's father or lord.

### FAMILY CEREMONIES

There are many ceremonies devoted to honoring older generations. One of the most important is an annual Buddhist festival called the Bon Matsuri or O'Bon, which has been held since the seventh century. On July 13, after thoroughly cleaning their houses, people go to family gravesites to invite

*View of an altar inside a Buddhist temple.*

## Golden Week

The Golden Week is a collection of several national holidays that occur within seven days in late April and early May. It begins with Green Day on April 29, which honors the birthday of Emperor Showa (1901–1989), also known as Hirohito. The term "green" refers to Hirohito's love of nature and the environment. Other Golden Week holidays are Constitution Day on May 3, which marks the day in 1947 when the new post–World War II constitution was put into effect; "Between Day" on May 4, created to make the week into a continuous holiday in combination with weekends; and Children's Day on May 5, which is also called the boy's festival. Other important annual festivals during the year—outside of Golden Week—include New Year's Day, Girl's Day on March 3, and Shichi-Go-San on November 15, when children ages 3, 5, and 7 are taken to pray at shrines because the Japanese believe that odd numbers are lucky.

the spirits of the dead to visit them, then lead the way home with a blazing lantern. From that time through the next two days, they act as though the spirits are among them, conversing with their dead relatives and offering them food. On July 15 they offer the spirits a farewell meal of rice dumplings and light a bonfire to help them find their way back to the afterlife.

Another ceremony that shows respect for the older generation takes place when a man is about to turn sixty years of age. At that time, he wears a traditional robe-like garment called a kimono and changes from a plain-colored one to a red one. This symbolizes the shedding of responsibility. From this point on, the man's family is expected to care for him.

Rituals take place at other significant points in life as well. The first special ceremony takes place three days after birth, when an infant is named in the presence of family members. At approximately one month of age, the family takes the baby to the nearest Shinto shrine, where the name is recorded by the priest to make the child an official member of the community.

Two other significant ceremonies are weddings and funerals. The marriage ceremony is usually Shinto, and the bride

*A Japanese bride dressed in a traditional kimono and headdress.*

and groom take tiny sips of sake, which is a rice wine, to mark their union. The bride dresses in an elaborately decorated kimono and wears an equally elaborate headdress. The groom might also wear a kimono, but it is becoming more common for him to wear an American-style suit. Sometimes the bride changes into an American-style wedding dress for the reception that follows the marriage ceremony.

A Japanese funeral is most often Buddhist, and in almost every case the deceased is cremated. First, however, the body is placed in a coffin with its head pointing north. After twenty-four hours, the coffin is carried to the crematorium, where priests say special prayers and family members burn incense to honor the deceased. Ashes are deposited in cemeteries beside family memorial stones.

Shinto funerals are similar to Buddhist ones, except that the head of the body must point east, and during cremation the priest not only prays but also tells about the person's life. Instead of burning incense, family members make offerings of paper and sacred twigs.

## HOUSES

Most homes have a family altar to honor the dead, where incense might be burned or special offerings made. Most houses also have a special alcove called a tokonoma that holds a painted scroll and a flower arrangement on a raised platform. This area is not connected with the dead but with the living; it is a place to appreciate beauty. Scholar Boye Lafayette De Mente explains:

> The custom of building *tokonoma* into Japanese homes and other buildings is an ancient one. It began as a private Buddhist altar . . . then developed into an integral part of the aesthetic practices that are a distinctive part of Japanese culture—practices that derive from Shintoistic themes that celebrate nature and humanity's relationship with the cosmos, and from Taoist and Buddhist teachings that the appreciation of nature and beauty is necessary for the whole person.[24]

The Japanese appreciation for nature is reflected in other aspects of their dwellings as well. For example, many houses have elaborate gardens with landscapes that include pools and bridges. Miniature landscapes are also created in garden boxes, dishes, or trays that can be brought inside. The art of cultivating dwarf trees for these landscapes, called bonsai, has become popular throughout the world.

Traditional Japanese houses have a series of sliding doors that allow a person to walk out into the garden with ease. During the day, these doors are usually left open. Constructed entirely of wood, houses are elevated about two feet off the ground on posts and have a porch along their sunniest side.

Inside the home, sliding panels made of wood and paper partition the rooms; there are rarely any permanent wall divisions. Ordinary dwellings are divided into a kitchen and up to four other rooms. Homes for the nobility have dozens of rooms. In either case, mats of woven straw or reeds cover the floors. To keep them clean, Japanese people always take off their shoes before entering a house.

In rural areas, kitchen floors are often earthen. Other rooms might have wood or reed mats. Walls are made of clay and straw, and cooking stoves are clay and brick. There is no inside plumbing; water for drinking comes from wells, and toilet facilities are some distance from the house.

Newer Japanese homes are one- or two-story prefabricated structures with steel frames. In late 1992, approximately 90 percent of all new houses were prefabricated, and this type of home continues to be popular. Built in large factories, prefabricated homes can be assembled on a site by just a few workers in only four hours. The reduced cost of such construction is partly responsible for the fact that over 60 percent of Japanese own their own homes.

In major cities, however, many people choose to rent an apartment or condominium. These buildings are modern, American-style high-rises with indoor plumbing

*Bonsai gardens are popular throughout Japan and the rest of the world.*

and other conveniences. But despite such facilities, residents might still choose to bathe in a public bathhouse.

Communal bathing is an important part of Japanese life. The bath is a place to soak and relax in extremely hot water; soaping and rinsing is done before stepping into the tub. In fact, no soap should ever get in the bathing water, either at public bathhouses or at home.

*Communal bathing, although sexually segregated, is an important part of Japanese life.*

Until the 1950s, groups of men and women bathed together without any sexual meaning, but American influences resulted in a law mandating that bathhouses be sexually segregated, and a wall now separates the men's bathing area from the women's in public bathhouses. However, in private homes, men and women still bathe together or sequentially, using the same water. Traditional bathtubs are made of earthenware or cedar, but modern American-style bathtubs are common as well.

There is no furniture in a Japanese home except for tables, storage chests, and dressers. There are no chairs or beds, although modern houses typically include televisions, stereo equipment, and computers. People sit on cushions called *zabutons* and sleep on cotton-filled mattresses called futons. Both the *zabutons* and the futons are stored inside wall closets when not in use, making each room multipurpose.

## FOOD AND CLOTHING

The Japanese sit on *zabutons* at a low table to eat meals. Boiled white rice appears at all three meals—breakfast, lunch, and dinner—along with other items, and the beverage is usually green tea and/or sake. A bean-paste soup called *misoshiru* is typically part of breakfast, as is a dish of pickled vegetables. Lunch includes salted fish and vegetables. Dinner offers fish, beef, pork, or chicken and vegetables; meat is usually fried, whereas fish is often served raw. Noodle dishes are a common snack.

Western foods are increasingly becoming a part of the Japanese diet, although many people eat them with chopsticks instead of forks and spoons. Eggs are now frequently consumed for breakfast, and American-style fast-food restaurants provide busy urban workers with lunch and dinner. Hamburgers are particularly popular, but so is sushi, a Japanese fast food made of fish and rice. Other fast foods include fried chicken, barbecued chicken on skewers, bowls of beef and rice or noodles, baked sweet potatoes and boiled corn sold from carts, and riceballs, which are balls of rice containing meat, vegetables, salmon, or plums.

Clothing is also a combination of the traditional and the modern. Most Japanese people dress like Americans, but kimonos are worn for special events and relaxing at home. Women wear ankle-length kimonos whose designs and colors depend on their age, marital status, and the event being attended, while men's kimonos are shorter, plainer, more casual, and more typically reserved for use inside the house. Kimonos are traditionally made of silk; cotton versions of the simplest kimonos are called *yukuta*.

The shoes traditionally worn with either kimonos or *yukuta* are either wooden clogs called geta or rubber or straw sandals called zori. At one time, women in kimonos also wore elaborate hairstyles, but now even with traditional

*Sushi, Japanese fast food made of fish and rice.*

dress, Japanese hairstyles are now no different from Western ones; the high, elaborate hairstyles that Japanese women used to favor are currently seen only on geisha.

### ENTERTAINMENT

Like many other aspects of Japanese culture, entertainment is a blend of the ancient and the modern. People enjoy contemporary music and movies but they also continue to attend traditional Japanese music, dance, and theater performances.

Traditional Japanese music does not sound like Western music because it does not employ Western musical scales. In addition, only simple wind, percussion, and string instruments are used in a musical composition, which might combine aspects of music from other Asian countries. For example, gagaku, a type of music that was introduced into Japan from China in the eighth century A.D., is a blend of forms from Korea, Manchuria, Persia, India, and Indochina. Gagaku is often accompanied by dance, whereupon it is called *bugaku*.

Many types of Japanese theater also incorporate dance. For example, Kabuki theater employs special actors trained from youth in dance, voice, and acrobatics. "Kabuki" is derived from *kabuku,* which means to frolic. It was first applied to the dances of a woman named O-Kuni in 1603. She adapted the works of another type of theater, the No, but made her movements sexually suggestive. Within a short time the leaders of Japan forbade women from appearing on the Kabuki stage, and the tradition of all-male Kabuki performers continues today.

Kabuki also restricts itself to plays written prior to approximately 1900. Many of these performances involve battle scenes, which are elaborately staged. Spectacular sets change right in front of the audience using a revolving stage and elevators that rise from and descend into the floor. Costumes are also frequently changed on stage. They are ornate and can weigh as much as forty pounds each. Music accompanies the performance, either played on stage or in a nearby room, and plays can last all day, from 11 A.M. until evening.

The No theater from which Kabuki was originally derived is very different from its successor. It involves a bare stage, and props are primitive. For example, a boat may be represented by a simple frame in the basic shape of a vessel. However, like Kabuki, men play all of the roles, wearing various masks to represent different characters. There are a total of 240 traditional No plays performed today, usually accompanied by drums, a flute, and a chorus of voices.

*Wooden clogs, called geta, are traditionally worn with kimonos.*

A third theater form is the Bunraku, which involves one or more narrators and several puppets. The largest of these puppets is approximately two-thirds the size of a human being, and each must be manipulated by three operators using a combination of hand-puppetry and marionette work. Although the puppeteers remain silent, the audience can see them throughout the play. The entire performance is accompanied by music from a banjo-like string instrument called the samisen, which is also the traditional instrument of the geisha.

## SPORTS AND HOBBIES

The Japanese also continue to participate in traditional sports and hobbies. The most popular activities are martial arts, which include sumo, judo, karate, kendo, and *kyudo*.

*Kabuki drama contains singing, dancing, and acrobatics.*

Sumo is a type of wrestling that originated as part of Shinto ceremonies, when it was believed to be the favorite entertainment of the gods. Around the seventh century, it became a spectator sport unconnected to religious worship, although its format retained certain rituals that take place before and after a match. During the match, two men in loincloths face each other on a raised platform within a circle of sand. To win the competition, a sumo wrestler must shove his opponent out of the ring or force some part of his body other than his feet onto the ground.

Sumo wrestlers begin training for their sport in their early teens, and throughout their lives they eat special foods to increase their weight, which is typically between 250 and 375

*A sumo wrestler typically weighs between 250 and 375 pounds.*

## A Foreign Sumo Champion

Sumo wrestler Akebono Taro is the first foreigner to become a Japanese sumo champion. Born in Hawaii in 1969, he was a student at Hawaii Pacific College when a Japanese sumo stable master, Azumazeki, spotted him and asked him to join his group of wrestlers. Akebono rose rapidly through the ranks, winning a series of competitions, and in 1993 he won the title of *Yokozuna,* sumo champion. At the same time, he had to learn the Japanese language in order to maintain the verbal traditions that accompany sumo wrestling. In 1996, Akebono became a Japanese citizen.

pounds. Today there are approximately seven hundred sumo wrestlers in Japan, distributed among twenty-eight stables that manage their careers.

Judo is also a form of fighting in which opponents try to throw one another to the floor, hold the other down, or lift the other into the air. However, most participants in these competitions are not as large as sumo wrestlers, and they use different techniques. The forerunner of judo, jujitsu, was developed as a form of unarmed one-on-one combat used by samurai warriors to defend themselves when taken unawares. Today judo is a form of mind and body discipline, rather than a means of battle. However, it is also a competitive sport and part of the Olympic Games.

Karate is another type of fighting, but it does not involve much body contact. Rather than grapple one another to the ground, opponents hit or kick each other. However, competitions of this type are rare. Instead, when two contestants face one another, they do not actually inflict any injuries but are judged on the quality of their offensive and defensive movements. Some types of competitions are individual demonstrations of karate skills; contestants perform set routines and are judged not only on the quality of their movements but on the shouts that must accompany them.

Kendo is a form of fencing that originated in the seventh or eighth century and was adopted in the sixteenth century as part of the training exercises for samurai warriors. At that time, combatants battled with heavy wooden staves, but since the eighteenth century they have used bamboo ones.

In competitions, kendoists wear a great deal of protective clothing, and they win by accumulating points that are earned through touching various body parts.

*Kyudo* is archery with bamboo bows and arrows. Hunters, warriors, and pirates were the original practitioners of *kyudo*, but today it is primarily a competitive sport. One form of competition is *yabusame*, during which archers shoot at stationary targets while galloping on horseback. *Yabusame* began as a Shinto rite related to the harvest, and it is still performed at certain Shinto festivals.

Another popular spectator sport in Japan is a Western one: baseball. Many Japanese also enjoy playing this sport themselves at one of more than ten thousand baseball and softball fields, more than four thousand of which are corporate-owned. The activity was introduced in Japan in 1873; the first professional teams appeared in 1934. The country has two leagues—the Central League and the Pacific League—each with six teams that play 130 games per season (April through October). At the end of the season, the leading team in each league competes in the Japan Series.

Other common outdoor activities are basketball, volleyball, tennis, bicycling, soccer, swimming, kite flying, and gardening. Indoor activities include ceramics, doll making, flower arranging, and board games. The three most popular games are go, *shogi*, and mahjong. Go and *shogi* are Chinese games that were introduced into Japan in the eighth century. To play go, two people take turns placing small stones on a gameboard in an attempt to capture as many squares as possible. *Shogi* is similar to chess, in that it uses pieces of various ranks to capture an opponent's king. Mahjong is a more complicated game in which four players earn points by combining 13 out of 136 ceramic tiles, each with a different character, into a winning hand. It is also a Chinese game, but was not introduced into Japan until the 1920s.

## THE MEDIA

Watching television and movies is another common activity. Japanese television is similar to American television, but programmers are not subjected to any censorship at all regarding sex, language, or violence. Movie producers experience the same level of freedom, and during the 1980s they created a glut of pornographic movies that damaged the international reputation of the Japanese film industry. Prior to that time, Japanese filmmakers were primarily known for creating popular science-fiction movies that remain cult classics today.

Newspapers and magazines are also uncensored. However, journalists do not have unrestricted access to news sources. They belong to press clubs, of which there are approximately four hundred in the country. Certain clubs cover certain sources, which include political parties, government offices, corporations, and police headquarters. For example, members of the club for foreign correspondents can only deal with the prime minister's office and the Foreign Ministry. This system has led foreign reporters to complain that they are being shut out of important news stories. Meanwhile, Japanese newspapers deal with the situation by employing a large number of reporters from different press clubs. None of these reporters receive individual credit for their stories, but they can expect to remain with the same newspaper for life.

There are currently 177 daily newspapers in Japan, 5 of which have ties to commercial television networks and are distributed nationally. The 3 largest newspapers—the *Yomiuri Shimbun*, the *Asahi Shimbun*, and the *Mainichi Shimbun*—have a combined circulation of 22 million people. There are also several English language newspapers in the country. Of these, the largest is *The Japan Times*, which employs many foreign writers and offers a unique perspective on Japanese issues.

Together these sources provide in-depth information about national and international issues. In addition, approximately 14 percent of Japanese television programming is devoted to news, and computers provide the Japanese with access to the global resources of the Internet. Therefore, although Japan maintains its ancient traditions, its people are well aware of the problems of their own country and the rest of the world.

# Governing for the Future

Although the Japanese culture maintains many ancient traditions, its constitution is essentially an American document, and most aspects of its government are either American or European in nature. Consequently some Japanese have called for a revamped political structure. Their suggestions have had little influence, largely because of the characteristic Japanese resistance to change.

## Ruling the Country

Japan's current constitution was enacted in 1947 as an amendment to the Meiji Constitution of 1889. Drafted by the occupying forces after World War II, the more recent document declared the emperor to be a mere symbol of the nation, thereby ending his status as divine ruler. As a result, the emperor's duties are now primarily ceremonial, and most Japanese are satisfied with this arrangement. In a 1995 survey, only 6 percent thought the emperor should be given more power. Only 8 percent wanted his position eliminated.

The true executive power is in the hands of the cabinet, led by the prime minister. No member of this body can belong to the military, and the cabinet must have the support of the chief legislative body, the Diet. If the Diet declares a lack of confidence in the cabinet, the cabinet's members must resign. Alternatively, the prime minister can dissolve the Diet, whereupon new elections are held to determine the Diet's members.

The Diet is comprised of two branches, the House of Representatives or lower house and the House of Councillors or upper house. The 252 members of the House of Councillors serve six-year terms; elections are staggered so that only half of the members are replaced every three years. One hundred are elected directly by voters, while 152 are assigned by political parties to represent individual prefects, based on the number of votes each party receives. The House of Representatives has 512 members representing specific districts. Once voted into office, they serve four-year terms.

Candidates for office are not allowed to canvas for votes by going door-to-door. Instead, they drive up and down streets talking on public address systems, providing they are not too loud (although this restriction is often ignored). Such publicity is important, because voters must write the name of the candidate on the ballot themselves. Any Japanese citizen age twenty years and older is eligible to vote, and most elections garner a voter turnout of over 90 percent. Women achieved the right to vote in 1945.

After each election, a new session of the Diet is officially opened by the emperor. The Diet meets in the National Diet

| POLITICAL GROUPS IN THE HOUSE OF REPRESENTATIVES | |
|---|---|
| | (as of April 13, 1999) |
| Liberal Democratic Party | 266 |
| Democratic Party of Japan | 93 |
| New Komeito and Reformers' Party | 52 |
| Liberal Party | 39 |
| Japanese Communist Party | 26 |
| Socialist Democratic Party | 14 |
| Mushozoku-no-kai | 2 |
| Sakigate | 2 |
| Independents | 6 |
| Incumbents | 500 |
| Vacancies | 0 |
| Membership | 500 |

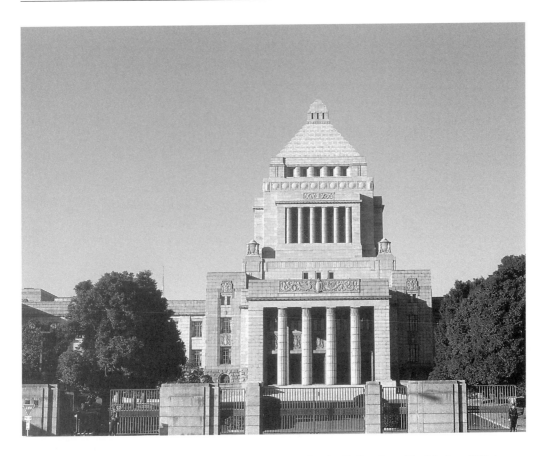

Building, in Tokyo near the Imperial Palace. The building's left wing is for the lower house, the right wing for the upper house. The prime minister lives in a residence behind the building, and the headquarters of the two most influential political parties in the country, the Liberal Democratic Party and the Japan Socialist Party, are nearby.

*The National Diet Building in Tokyo.*

Once the Diet is in session, both houses meet independently to vote on whether a particular bill will become law. When both houses are in agreement, the vote is final. However, if the upper house rejects a bill that has been approved by the lower house, it can subsequently vote to override upper house opposition with just a two-thirds majority. The lower house can also ratify a treaty or name a prime minister on its own with just a simple majority. Generally, prime ministers are members of the party with the largest number of members in the Diet.

There are several other governing bodies in Japan besides the Diet, all functioning at the local level much like their national counterparts to make laws and budgets. Each town or city has a one-house legislature with an assembly and a mayor. Each prefecture has a one-house legislature with an assembly and a governor.

Japan is divided into forty-seven prefectures of varying size. The smallest geographically, which encompasses the city of Osaka, is 720 square miles; the largest, which is comprised of the entire island of Hokkaido, is 32,246 square miles. The most heavily populated prefecture is Tokyo, which is divided further into governmental units called wards, each of which has its own chief and assembly. All major cities with populations of five hundred thousand or more are so divided. Other cities with wards include Yokohama, Osaka, Kyoto, Kobe, and Hiroshima.

## POLITICAL INFLUENCE

Political parties have a great deal of influence at all levels of Japanese government. From the end of World War II until 1989, the dominant party, the Liberal Democratic Party, had almost no opposition, but today there are many diverse parties representing specialized interests. They include the Japan Socialist Party, the Democratic Socialist Party, the Japan Communist Party, and the New Liberal Club. Most parties are loosely grouped; memberships rise and fall dramatically as political alliances change, and groups are often reorganized.

Individuals within each group typically hold more political power than the group itself. Businesses donate large amounts of money to these people, who then decide how the money should be spent. This system has given rise to a great deal of political corruption. Many Japanese have called for the banning of corporate political contributions in order to eliminate the possibility of bribery. Although such a policy has not yet been adopted, a series of contribution reforms were enacted in the mid-1990s. Under these reforms, a business or other group was restricted to contributing no more than $50,000 to an election campaign, and candidates were required to report all contributions to the government. Elected officials who are discovered to have disobeyed election laws lose their positions and are banned from running for another office for five years.

Political power is also wielded by the country's twelve ministries: Agriculture, Construction, Education, Finance,

## HIROHITO

Emperor of Japan from 1926 until 1989, Michi-nomiya Hirohito was the longest-reigning monarch in Japanese history. He is also known as Emperor Showa, after the name of his reigning period, "Showa," which means "Enlightened Peace." Hirohito was born on April 29, 1901, in Tokyo. As a young man, he took an interest in marine biology and wrote several books on the subject. In 1921 he became the first Japanese crown prince to travel abroad when he visited Europe. As emperor, he led his nation into World War II, although some historians have suggested he was not himself in favor of the conflict, but merely yielded to the wishes of powerful members of his government. Hirohito also helped his country adjust to defeat and subsequent occupation by American forces. During the 1950s, he personalized the position of emperor by making numerous public appearances and revealing details about his family life; previous emperors had remained cloistered. In 1971 he again traveled to Europe, and in 1975 to the United States. When he died on January 7, 1989, he was succeeded by his oldest son, Crown Prince Akihito, who in 1959 became the first Japanese prince to marry a commoner, Shoda Michiko.

Foreign Affairs, Forestry and Fisheries, Health and Welfare, Home Affairs, International Trade and Industry, Justice, Labor, and Transport. Each of these bureaucracies is headed by a different cabinet member and has the ability to establish policies that control many aspects of Japanese life.

## MEDICAL CARE

The Ministry of Health and Welfare manages the country's medical policies, oversees its health centers and national health insurance program, and establishes the amount of money a doctor involved in this program can charge for a procedure. At one time, patients in the program received free medical care, but as of 1984 every person has had to pay at least 10 percent of their expenses, and participants in the program must pay a monthly premium. However, employers are required to provide workers with health insurance to help defray medical costs, and the country offers additional forms of assistance to the poor.

Approximately 97 percent of all health care in the country is administered through the national health program at clinics and hospitals. But regardless of program participation, physicians who are not on the staff of a particular hospital are not allowed to treat their own patients there. Consequently many doctors perform advanced medical procedures in their clinics and send patients to a hospital only in extreme cases.

However, a person can walk into a hospital and request admission without a doctor's referral. Emergency rooms are usually only open in the evening, though, and some hospitals do not have them at all. Most patients must go through a regular admissions process, and the wait can be extremely long. Once admitted, patients must provide many of their own supplies, including soap and towels, and their relatives are encouraged not only to visit them but also to assist in their care.

Medical treatments include conventional Western techniques as well as acupuncture, which is the insertion of needles into "energy points" on the body. A Chinese practice, acupuncture was brought to Japan in the sixth century. Today it is performed not only by private physicians but also by doctors in major medical centers, hospitals, and universities.

Abortion is also common in Japan, although the number of procedures has been decreasing steadily since the 1950s, when an average of 4 million a year were performed. Today that figure is less than five hundred thousand. Abortion is legal and relatively easy to obtain, because by law, anyone who cannot afford a baby is entitled to an abortion.

## COURTS AND GOVERNMENT AGENCIES

Laws are enforced by a legal system headed by the Supreme Court, which has one chief justice and fourteen associate justices appointed by the cabinet, as well as approximately twenty research assistants. At the time of appointment, the House of Representatives can vote to reject a particular justice. Those who serve on the Court must be at least forty years old and retire at age seventy.

In addition to the Supreme Court, there are eight high courts, fifty district courts, fifty family courts, and dozens of summary courts. Family courts deal with issues such as divorce and child custody, while summary courts deal with minor cases involving small sums of money. As with many aspects of Japanese government, the legal system functions much like the system in the United States.

Japan also has nine administrative agencies that handle government affairs. Under the control of the prime minister, they are the Administrative Management Agency, the Defense Agency, the Economic Planning Agency, the Environmental Agency, the Hokkaido Development Agency, the National Land Agency, the National Public Safety Commission, the Science and Technology Agency, and the Okinawa Development Agency.

In addition, the country has a voluntary army, navy, and air force called the National Self-Defense Force, which has gained much economic and public support in recent years. The right of Japan to have military forces has often been questioned, because the country's constitution, as established by the Americans after World War II, specifically forbids it. However, the document states that Japan cannot maintain armed forces for *aggressive* purposes. Therefore in 1959 the Japanese Supreme Court ruled that the Self-Defense Forces could exist because the organization is entirely defensive in nature, and the United States has supported this decision.

The United States has pledged to protect Japan and operates several military bases there, but the Japanese still feel they need their own soldiers. According to a 1978 survey, 56

## LAFCADIO HEARN

Journalist Lafcadio Hearn is considered by Japanese to be the first Westerner to understand their attitudes and culture thoroughly. Born in 1850, Hearn became a newspaper reporter in the United States before moving to Japan in 1890. Shortly thereafter he began to write articles about the Japanese people for two American magazines, *Atlantic Monthly* and *Harper's*. He subsequently married a Japanese woman, changed his name to Koizumi Yakumo, became a naturalized citizen, taught English and literature in several Japanese universities, and wrote numerous books that helped Westerners understand Japan, including *Japan: An Attempt at Interpretation* (1904) and *A Japanese Miscellany* (1904). Hearn died in 1904.

percent of the people felt that the United States would not sufficiently aid the Japanese if they were attacked by a foreign power. In the same survey, 71 percent of the people wanted the constitution changed to permit a more aggressive military. However, the country is strongly antinuclear, and experts believe that even though Japan has the knowledge to develop its own nuclear weapons within two years, its populace will not allow it to do so.

## A Difficult Relationship with China

Antinuclear sentiment might change, however, because several of Japan's neighbors—most notably North Korea, China, Pakistan, and India—have been developing nuclear weapons. Japan's relationship with these countries has been difficult in recent years, but it has increasingly tried to reach out to them.

In late 1998, for example, the Japanese government invited Chinese President Jiang Zemin to Japan in an attempt to mend the relationship between the two countries; he was the first Chinese leader to visit Japan since World War II. However, the visit did not go well. Although Zemin and Japanese prime minister Keizo Obuchi drafted a declaration of partnership, the two leaders failed to sign it after Obuchi made what Zemin considered an insincere apology for atrocities committed by the Japanese during their occupation of China from 1931 to 1945.

In rejecting Obuchi's apology, Zemin said, "In Japan, there are still certain people, and people in high positions, who constantly distort history to try to beautify aggression. This continues to hurt the feelings of Chinese people and other people. . . . It is important that you squarely face that history and learn a lesson from it."[25]

But political experts believe that Japanese officials have been avoiding a more strongly worded apology for fear that it will make Japan liable to claims for economic compensation for the atrocities. At the same time, cultural experts point out that the Japanese often try to "save face" by avoiding the appearance that they have done anything dishonorable.

However, the two countries will most likely find a way to mend their differences because they are becoming increasingly dependent upon one another in the economic realm. Japan is Asia's chief source of financial aid and investment, which means that China needs Japan's help in order to develop its economy. Meanwhile, Japan wants closer ties with China because its own economy is faltering and because China would be a welcome ally in struggles with other Asian countries such as North Korea.

## INTERNAL THREATS

Japan has long been concerned about threats from other countries. However, some of Japan's most serious threats in recent years have come from within. Overpopulation, environmental pollution, and government corruption have all been sources of concern, but domestic terrorism has been perhaps the most troubling problem in the country.

In March 1995, members of a Japanese cult, Aum Shinrikyo, placed plastic bags filled with diluted sarin, a lethal chemical, on crowded Tokyo subway trains during rush hour;

*Japan's prime minister, Keizo Obuchi.*

twelve people were killed and over five thousand injured. In subsequent months, the same group put bags of other chemicals, including cyanide gas, in other subway stations, and several more people became ill. When cult members eventually were arrested, police discovered a variety of chemicals and biological weapons in their possession and concluded that the group had been planning a more serious attack on Tokyo.

Consequently the Diet passed several laws to make it more difficult to own or make sarin and other chemical weapons. In addition, several members of the group were convicted for their involvement in the crimes. But many of them served little time in prison, and the cult attempted to reorganize.

Moreover, domestic terrorism continued to plague Japan. For example, in April 1998 someone removed the bolts from the track of a high-speed train. After the act failed to cause serious harm, anonymous letters were sent threatening to kill more than ten thousand people via train derailments

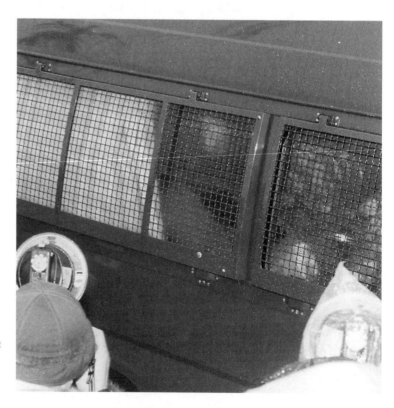

*Leader of the Aum Shinrikyo cult, Shoko Asahara, is arrested as a suspect in the Tokyo subway poison gas attack.*

throughout the country. The police suspect that the responsibility for the bolt removals and the letters lay with the Kakumaru-ha, an ultraradical Marxist group. The Kakumaru-ha opposes the current government and believes that the Japanese police and the media conspire to distort the truth about a variety of issues.

In the late 1990s there were twenty ultraradical leftist groups in Japan, with approximately thirty thousand members. One of the largest and most militant of these groups, Chukaku-Ha, opposed the imperial system as well as Japan's ties with Western nations. Its members participated in mass street demonstrations and occasionally destroyed public and private property with bombs, rockets, and other incendiary devices.

## FOREIGN INFLUENCE

Many less radical groups have also criticized the nature of Japan's relationship with Western nations. For example, Peter Popham and Bradley Winterton, two British authors who live in Japan and write about its issues, say, "Many Japanese, even among the young, complain that spiritual qualities have been sacrificed in the postwar rush to catch up with the West."[26] In fact, a 1986 survey indicated that while 70 percent of Japanese wanted more exposure to Western news, technology, and products, only 30 percent wanted more personal contact with foreigners. Moreover, although Japan belongs to the United Nations, it often refuses to join other nations in foreign aid projects for less fortunate countries, and it turned down American requests for Japanese assistance during the Persian Gulf War in 1990 and 1991.

However, the increasingly global nature of communication is now making it difficult for the Japanese to avoid contact with outsiders. As a result, there are signs that American influences are changing some of the most fundamental characteristics of Japanese culture. For example, the traditional Japanese reticence toward sharing personal information is beginning to crumble. In May 1999, Associated Press correspondent Joseph Coleman reported that the Japanese are now increasingly revealing details about their private lives on television talk shows and Internet chat rooms, adding: "A traditional emphasis on keeping up appearances has long made the public baring of troubles taboo. And in a society that demands self-effacement, talking about yourself can be seen as unbearably boorish. The shrinking violet approach, however, is slowly losing its appeal."[27] Coleman quotes Japanese author Maguro Shimonoseki, who has been tracking this trend, as saying: "In the past, Japanese considered not being assertive a virtue. Now, more people are thinking it's okay to say what's on their minds."[28]

### LOSS OF PRIVACY

The Japanese are giving up privacy in other ways as well. For example, the country's National Police Agency (NPA) has instituted the N (for "number") system, which uses computerized monitors to record the license numbers of cars on particular roads. The NPA says that this system makes it easier to find stolen cars and missing persons and eliminates unnecessary roadblocks. Another threat to privacy is a proposed national number identification system, which would assign every Japanese citizen a ten-digit number and create a cen-

*American influences are changing some of the fundamental characteristics of Japanese culture.*

---

## MODERN RECYCLING

In recent years, environmentalism has become extremely important to the Japanese, and trash recycling programs are prevalent throughout the country. In major cities, people set their aluminum cans and glass bottles outside twice a month for recycling. They also save their newspapers for two or three weeks, giving them to the driver of the *chirigami koukan* truck in exchange for a roll of toilet paper. However, Japan does not currently recycle its chopsticks, a failure that has been criticized by Japanese environmentalists.

---

tral database of personal information about each individual. There are already other systems in place to organize drivers' license numbers and tax information, but the new system would go beyond its predecessors in scope and ease of access.

Experts in Japanese culture believe that the Japanese people are willing to accept such limitations on personal freedom as long as the government has demonstrated that they are for the good of the country. In an article on privacy issues in Japan, Stephen Osmond points out that the Japanese do not place as much importance on individuality as Americans. He explains:

> Adherence to public norms and the "group mentality" is an overriding feature of Japanese life. The sense of what is proper in personal and public conduct and concepts of "face" (personal honor and dignity), freedom, and privacy are all informed by group sensibilities to a degree that far exceeds Western interpretations. Even the U.S.-style constitution adopted immediately after World War II reflected this concern: Article Thirteen promised that the individual's pursuit of life, liberty, and happiness would be the supreme consideration "to the extent that it does not interfere with the public welfare." Responsibility to the public good supersedes an individual's "rights."[29]

## MY WAY-ISM

Increasingly, young Japanese are asserting their individuality in decidedly Western ways. They are no longer as eager to lose themselves in a company identity or to sacrifice their lives to care for their elders. Stephen Osmond reports:

> As Japan's population grows older—life expectancy is now in the upper seventies as compared with the low fifties at the start of this century—the formal demands of filial piety and shared living conditions have simply become an impractical burden. The urban economy gives younger people a chance to set up independent homes and lifestyles, and they seize the opportunity eagerly. This growing independence (and perceived isolation) of young adults gives many Japanese a considerable sense of unease. Young people are frequently criticized for selfishness and for adopting "Western" standards, and common euphemisms like "My Way-ism" and "My Home-ism" are applied to new trends that emphasize personal independence and materialism at the expense of traditional values and ties.[30]

At the same time, Osmond believes that Japanese self-identity is too rooted in the group for people to become too individualistic. Moreover, the Japanese culture has withstood other assaults from foreign influences without losing its cohesiveness. When such stresses threaten the traditional Japanese way of life, the country tends to isolate itself psychologically if not physically from outsiders, to revive its traditional attitudes, and to strengthen national unity.

However, it remains to be seen whether Japan will be able to continue this approach. As David H. Hunsberger points out in a review of the book *Japan's Quest: The Search for International Role, Recognition, and Respect,* edited by Warren S. Hunsberger:

> Japan's basic strategy since the mid–nineteenth century has been to seek attractive foreign models, select, copy, adopt, and adapt. Phenomenal achievements have resulted. But now that Japan has caught up, there is a dearth of foreign models. Japan is approaching the twenty-first century with much reduced confidence. Its consensus society is not well prepared to deal with the unknown or unexpected.
>
> The Japanese people have not squarely faced the implications and obligations of vast economic power, nor

# HONDA

While entrepreneurship is not highly valued in Japan today, it was the foundation of many modern Japanese corporations. The Honda automotive company is a case in point. Honda began as a small business run by Honda Soichiro (1906–1991), a blacksmith's son who did automotive repair and made pistons for the Toyota Motor Corporation, which itself began as a family-run textile manufacturing company. During World War II, Honda made pistons and other devices for the military, and after the war he became interested in making motorcycles. In 1946 he founded the Honda Institute of Technology to develop small, efficient engines. In 1948 the institute became the Honda Motor Company, which soon became a leading motorcycle manufacturer. When Honda's

motorcycles proved unable to beat European ones in racing competitions, its engineers took apart European bikes, studied them, and altered Honda bikes to make them superior. Honda subsequently took the same approach to manufacturing automobiles, developing a car that got better gas mileage than existing ones. Today the company is a leading producer of automobiles, motorcycles, and farm machinery.

*Honda Soichiro (standing) is congratulated after a successful test run.*

the need to devote resources and attention to keeping peace in an increasingly interconnected world. These failures reflect lingering Japanese insularity and the trauma of defeat in World War II, and a strong residual dependence on the United States. . . .[31]

In summarizing the book, David Hunsberger notes that Japan is not a world leader, despite its prominence. He argues that in order to succeed in the future, the country must become more deeply involved in global issues and make solid contributions to international problem-solving efforts.

However, this will require Japan to change some of its most basic characteristics. In the past, such changes have not come easily, and it remains to be seen whether the country will be able to rise to the challenge. But if it does—if it is able to become a leader rather than a follower, and put aside its resistance to relationships with foreigners—Japan could become a strong force for positive progress in the twenty-first century.

# Facts About Japan

## Geography

Area: 145,882 square miles

Coastline: 18,487 miles

Climate: Ranges from tropical in the south to cool temperate in the north

Terrain: Primarily mountainous

Highest point: Mount Fuji, 12,388 feet

Land use (1993): arable land—11 percent; permanent crops and pastures—3 percent; forests and woodland—67 percent; other—19 percent

## People

Population (1998): 125,931,533

Age structure (1998):

0–14 years old—15 percent; 9,802,921 male, 9,342,254 female

15–64 years old—69 percent; 43,486,840 male, 43,135,979 female

65 and older—16 percent; 8,388,242 male, 11,775,297 female

Population growth rate (1998): 0.2 percent

Birth rate (1998): 10.26 births/1,000 population

Death rate (1998): 7.94 deaths/1,000 population

Fertility rate (1998): 1.46 children born/woman

Ethnic groups: 99.4 percent Japanese; 0.6 percent other

Religions: Shinto and Buddhist 84 percent; Other 16 percent

Literacy: 99 percent of population

Voting: Universal suffrage, beginning at age 20

## Economy

Unemployment rate (1997): 3.4 percent

Number of workers (1997): 67.23 million

Occupation of workers (1994): trade and services—50 percent; manufacturing, mining, and construction—33 percent; utilities and communication—7 percent; agriculture, forestry, and fishing—6 percent; government—3 percent

Currency: Yen

## Government

Capital: Tokyo

Government type: constitutional monarchy

## ARMED FORCES

Military branches: Japan Ground Self-Defense Force (army); Japan Maritime Self-Defense Force (navy); Japan Air Self-Defense Force (air force)

Minimum age for military service: 18

Number of ships in merchant marine: 738

## INFRASTRUCTURE

Railways: 14,708.3 miles of rail, mostly electrified

Highways: 994,200 miles, of which 534,105 are paved

Airports: 167 as of 1997

Major ports and harbors: 21

# NOTES

### INTRODUCTION: A UNIFIED PEOPLE

1. Quoted in Richard Tames, *A Traveller's History of Japan.* Brooklyn, NY: Interlink Books, 1993, p. 207.

2. Boye Lafayette De Mente, *Japan Encyclopedia.* Lincolnwood, IL: Passport Books, 1995, p. v.

3. De Mente, *Japan Encyclopedia,* p. 114.

### CHAPTER 1: THE IMPACT OF GEOGRAPHY

4. Tames, *A Traveller's History,* p. 6.

5. Quoted in Tames, *A Traveller's History,* p. 8.

### CHAPTER 2: FOREIGNERS AS ENEMIES AND REFORMERS

6. De Mente, *Japan Encyclopedia,* p. 481.

7. Peter Popham and Bradley Winterton, *Traveler's JAPAN Companion.* Switzerland: Kummerly + Frey AG, 1998, p. 96.

8. Edwin O. Reischauer, *The Japanese.* Cambridge, MA: Belknap Press of Harvard University Press, 1977, pp. 72–73.

9. Reischauer, *The Japanese,* p. 70.

10. Tames, *A Traveller's History,* pp. 173–74.

### CHAPTER 3: A PEOPLE OF INDUSTRY

11. Quoted in Mark Magnier, "The Resistance to Change Is Rooted in Postwar Success," *Los Angeles Times,* April 15, 1999, p. C14.

12. Magnier, "The Resistance to Change," p. C1.

13. Quoted in Magnier, "The Resistance to Change," p. C14.

14. Magnier, "The Resistance to Change," p. C14.

15. Quoted in Mark Magnier, "Entrepreneurship Hits a Cultural Wall," *Los Angeles Times,* April 15, 1999, p. C1.

16. Quoted in John Langone, "The Rising Tide of Violence Among Japanese Youth," *Asia,* November/December 1983, p. 12.

17. Quoted in Magnier, "Entrepreneurship," p. C14.

18. Magnier, "Entrepreneurship," p. C14.

19. Popham and Winterton, *Traveler's JAPAN Companion*, p. 95.

20. De Mente, *Japan Encyclopedia*, p. 129.

## CHAPTER 4: AN ANCIENT CULTURE IN MODERN TIMES

21. Paul Watt, "Shinto and Buddhism: Wellsprings of Japanese Spirituality," *Asia Society's Focus on Asian Studies*, vol. 2, no. 1, *Asian Religions*, Fall 1982, p. 21. www.askasia.org/frclasrm/readings/r000009.htm.

22. Popham and Winterton, *Traveler's JAPAN Companion*, p. 104.

23. Watt, "Shinto and Buddhism," p. 21.

24. De Mente, *Japan Encyclopedia*, p. 185.

## CHAPTER 5: GOVERNING FOR THE FUTURE

25. Quoted in Knight Ridder Newspapers, "Chinese Leader Rebukes Japan on WWII Past," *Dallas Morning News*, November 29, 1998, p. 14A.

26. Popham and Winterton, *Traveler's JAPAN Companion*, p. 91.

27. Joseph Coleman/Associated Press, "Japanese Expose 'Private' Issues," *Ventura County Star*, May 8, 1999, p. A7.

28. Quoted in Coleman, "Japanese Expose 'Private' Issues," p. A7.

29. Stephen Osmond, "Part of a Group: Conforming in Japan," *The World & I*, vol. 12, June 1, 1997, p. 210.

30. Osmond, "Part of a Group," p. 210.

31. David Hunsberger, review of *Japan's Quest: The Search for International Role, Recognition, and Respect*, edited by Warren S. Hunsberger. www.hunsberger.org/quest.htm.

# CHRONOLOGY

**660 B.C.**
According to legend, Japan's first emperor, Jimmu ("divine warrior"), ascends the throne.

**A.D. 300**
The rule of the Yamato family begins.

**538–552**
Buddhism is introduced to Japan by visiting Koreans.

**645**
The Fujiwara clan becomes powerful at court.

**702**
Japan's first constitution is adopted.

**710**
The city of Nara becomes the first permanent capital of Japan.

**784**
The capital is moved to Nagaokakyo.

**794**
The capital is moved to Kyoto.

**884**
Japan cuts off all relations with China.

**1002–1019**
*The Tale of Genji* is written.

**1192**
The Kamakura Shogunate is established.

**1274**
The Mongols invade Japan.

**1338**
The Ashikaga Shogunate is established.

**1543**
The first Portuguese ship reaches Japan.

**1549**
The Roman Catholic missionary Francis Xavier begins preaching in Japan.

**1585**
Toyotomi Hideyoshi gains control of the country.

**1592**
Toyotomi Hideyoshi orders the invasion of Korea.

**1603**
The Tokugawa Shogunate is established.

**1637–1638**
Christian persecution becomes aggressive.

**1639**
Japan is officially closed to foreigners, except for Dutch traders at one Japanese port.

**1853**
Commodore Matthew Perry's ships reach Japan.

**1854**
Japan signs its first treaty with the United States.

**1867**
The Tokugawa Shogunate ends.

**1868**
The Emperor Meiji assumes the throne and begins modernizing the country.

**1868–1912**
The reforms of the Meiji period are implemented.

**1889**
A new constitution is adopted.

**1894–1895**
Japan is at war with China.

**1904–1905**

Japan is at war with Russia.

**1910**

Japan takes over Korea.

**1923**

A major earthquake strikes Tokyo and Yokohama.

**1931**

Japan takes over Manchuria.

**1941**

Japan attacks American forces in Pearl Harbor, Hawaii, involving the United States in World War II.

**1945**

The United States drops atomic bombs on Japan, which then surrenders.

**1945–1952**

Allied forces occupy Japan.

**1952**

Japan regains its independence, with restrictions.

**1964**

The International Olympic Games are held in Japan.

**1965**

Japan signs a peace treaty with South Korea.

**1972**

The United States returns the island of Okinawa to Japan, which it occupied after World War II; Japan reestablishes relations with China.

**1989**

Emperor Hirohito dies and is succeeded by Crown Prince Akihito.

**1990**

Japan develops economic problems.

**1994–1995**
Scandals related to political and financial corruption cause turmoil in the Japanese government.

**1995**
Several nerve gas attacks occur in Tokyo subways; members of a Japanese cult are convicted of the crime.

**1999**
The Japanese prime minister visits the United States to discuss the global economy.

# SUGGESTIONS FOR FURTHER READING

## BOOKS

Sawako Ariyoshi, *The Twilight Years.* Translated by Mildred Tahara. New York: Kodansha America, 1987. This Japanese novel deals with the problems of ageism and feminism in modern Japan.

Rhonda Blumberg, *Commodore Perry in the Land of the Shogun.* New York: Lothrop, Lee, and Shepard Books, 1985. This book for young adults provides insights into American navy commander Matthew Perry's role in opening Japan to trade during the 1850s.

Shusaku Endo, *Silence.* New York: Taplinger, 1980. This Japanese historical novel deals with the persecution of Christians during the 1600s.

Sheila Hamanaka (photographer) and Ayano Ohmi (calligrapher), *In Search of the Spirit: The Living National Treasures of Japan.* New York: Morrow Junior Books, 1999. This book for readers of all ages presents information about six traditional Japanese arts and crafts through interviews with a kimono artist, a bamboo weaver, a puppet master, a sword maker, a No actor, and a potter, each of whom have been designated a Living National Treasure by the Japanese government.

Kenneth Januszewski, *Beyond Sushi, A Year in Japan.* Phoenix, AZ: Colken Publishers, 1998. Januszewski describes life in Japan through the eyes of a Westerner.

John Langone, *In the Shogun's Shadow: Understanding a Changing Japan.* Boston: Little, Brown & Company, 1994. This book for young people discusses modern life in Japan and includes many first-person quotes from ordinary Japanese people.

Stewart Ross, *Causes and Consequences of the Rise of Japan and the Pacific Rim.* Austin, TX: Raintree Steck-Vaughn, 1996. This book for young adults explains the rapid growth of the Japanese economy after World War II, focusing primarily on the years from 1960 to 1995.

Murasaki Shikubu, *Genji monogatori (The Tale of the Genji).* The first Japanese novel, and perhaps the first novel in the world, this tenth-century book has been reprinted in several different editions using different translations, most notably a 1960 Modern Library edition with translation by Arthur Waley, a 1985 edition published by Vintage Books with translation by Edward G. Seidensticker, and a 1992 Knopf "Everyman's Library" edition.

## WEBSITES

**The CIA World Factbook 1998: Japan** (www.odci.gov/cia/ publications/factbook/ja.html). Provided by the U.S. Central Intelligence Agency, this online factbook offers current statistics about Japan.

**Japan** (www.math.uic.edu/~dturk/japan.html). Maintained by David Turkington, a member of the unofficial UIC-Japan Friendship Association at the University of Illinois at Chicago, this website offers information and photographs related to Japan and its people.

**Schauwecker's Guide to Japan** (www.japan-guide.com). This address is the website of *Schauwecker's Guide to Japan* and has more than two hundred searchable pages with illustrations and general information about Japan.

**Kids' Japan** (www.kids-japan.com). This website has a learning game for children that offers interesting facts about Japan.

# WORKS CONSULTED

Joseph Coleman/Associated Press, "Japanese Expose 'Private' Issues," *Ventura County Star,* May 8, 1999. This article discusses a growing tendency in Japan to share intimate details about one's life in public; formerly such discussions were considered taboo.

Boye Lafayette De Mente, *Japan Encyclopedia.* Lincolnwood, IL: Passport Books, 1995. Written by someone who once lived in Japan, this reference book provides many details about Japanese life.

David Hunsberger (www.hunsberger.org/quest.htm). This website reviews a book on the future of Japan, entitled *Japan's Quest: The Search for International Role, Recognition, and Respect,* edited by Warren S. Hunsberger of the U.S. Department of State.

Knight Ridder Newspapers, "Chinese Leader Rebukes Japan on WWII Past," *Dallas Morning News,* November 29, 1998. This article explains the bitterness that still exists among the Chinese people because of atrocities committed by Japan during World War II.

John Langone, "The Rising Tide of Violence Among Japanese Youth," *Asia,* November/December 1983. This article discusses the problem of teen violence in Japanese society.

Mark Magnier, "Entrepreneurship Hits a Cultural Wall," *Los Angeles Times,* April 15, 1999. Written by a business reporter, this article discusses the difficulties of being an entrepreneur in Japan.

———, "The Resistance to Change Is Rooted in Postwar Success," *Los Angeles Times,* April 15, 1999. Written by a business reporter, this article discusses the need for Japanese corporations to change their approach to business and the reasons why they will find such change difficult.

Stephen Osmond, "Part of a Group: Conforming in Japan," *The World & I.* Vol. 12, June 1, 1997. This article discusses the emphasis on conformity that is so prevalent in Japanese culture.

Peter Popham and Bradley Winterton, *Traveler's JAPAN Companion*. Switzerland: Kummerly + Frey AG, 1998. Intended for people who will be visiting Japan, this guidebook has photographs of Japanese sights as well as information about attractions, activities, and everyday life.

Edwin O. Reischauer, *The Japanese*. Cambridge, MA: Belknap Press of Harvard University Press, 1977. This lengthy book provides an in-depth discussion of various aspects of Japanese attitudes and culture.

Richard Tames, *A Traveller's History of Japan*. Brooklyn, NY: Interlink Books, 1993. This book offers a brief summation of Japanese history, from ancient times to the early 1990s.

Paul Watt, "Shinto and Buddhism: Wellsprings of Japanese Spirituality," *Asia Society's Focus on Asian Studies*. Vol. 2. No. 1. *Asian Religions,* Fall 1982, p. 21. This article offers an in-depth discussion of Japanese religious beliefs. www.askasia.org/frclasrm/readings/r000009.htm.

# INDEX

# PICTURE CREDITS

Cover photo: © Tony Stone Images/Chad Ehlers
AP/Wide World Photos, 53
Archive Photos, 31, 62, 64
Archive Photos/Popperfotos, 89
© Smithsonian Institute, 38
Corbis-Bettmann, 21
Corbis/Paul Thompson, 77
Corbis/Michael S. Yamashita, 55, 66
Digital Stock, 11, 18, 37, 61
FPG International, 29, 36, 49, 52, 59, 65, 69, 70
North Wind Picture Archives, 25, 27, 35
PhotoDisc, 6, 68
Reuters/Toshiyuko Aizawa/Archive Photos, 47
Reuters/Ken Igo/Archive Photos, 71
Reuters/Kimimasa Mayama/Archive Photos, 83
Reuters/John Pryke/Archive Photos, 45
Reuters/Eriko Sugita/Archive Photos, 17, 84
Reuters/Susumu Takahashi/Archive Photos, 86

# About the Author

Patricia D Netzley received her bachelor's degree in English from the University of California at Los Angeles (UCLA). After graduation she worked as an editor at the UCLA Medical Center, where she produced hundreds of medical articles, speeches, and pamphlets.

Netzley became a freelance writer in 1986. She is the author of several books for children and adults, including *The Assasination of President John F Kennedy* (Macmillan/New Discovery Books, 1994), *Alien Abductions* (Greenhaven Press, 1996), *Issues in the Environment* (Lucent Books, 1998), and the forthcoming *Encyclopedia of Environmental Literature* (ABC-CLIO)

Netzley's hobbies are weaving knitting, and needlework. She and her husband, Raymond, live in Southern California with their three children, Matthew, Sarah, and Jacob.